I am no more than half a block away from Aunt Rachel's bakery when the sense of dread I have been feeling suddenly grows larger.

It's obvious something is wrong, for a small congregation of shopkeepers, some still wearing their aprons, has gathered in the middle of the gutter. . . . As I draw nearer, I realize that a yellow scroll is plastered crookedly to the outside of each shop window. "JUDEN," it says, big bold black letters on yellow background. The sign means, "This shop is owned by Jews."

A Background Note about
The Story of Blima: A Holocaust Survivor

The heroine of this story, Blima Weisstuch, was a real person. She lived in Poland during World War II and the time known as the Holocaust, when millions of Jews and other people were imprisoned and killed by Adolf Hitler and his Nazi party. This part of Blima's story takes place between the years 1936 and 1947.

Eventually Blima and her husband moved to the United States, where they had a daughter and a son. *The Story of Blima: A Holocaust Survivor* is taken from a longer work written by Blima's daughter, Shirley Russak Wachtel. That longer story, which tells more of Blima's life in America, is entitled *My Mother's Shoes*.

SHIRLEY RUSSAK WACHTEL

THE STORY OF
BLIMA

A Holocaust Survivor

Introduction by Beth Johnson

 THE TOWNSEND LIBRARY

THE STORY OF BLIMA
A Holocaust Survivor

TP **THE TOWNSEND LIBRARY**

For more titles in the Townsend Library,
visit our website: **www.townsendpress.com**

All new material in this edition is
copyright © 2005 by Townsend Press.
Printed in the United States of America

0 9 8 7 6 5

Illustrations © 2005 by Hal Taylor

Townsend Press, Inc.
439 Kelley Drive
West Berlin, New Jersey 08091
cs@townsendpress.com

ISBN-13: 978-1-59194-051-7
ISBN-10: 1-59194-051-6

Library of Congress Control Number:
2005925111

CONTENTS

PART III: DAYLIGHT

INTRODUCTION

The Story of Blima. A Holocaust Survivor is a true story. It tells of the experience of Blima Weisstuch, a Jewish girl in Poland, between the years 1936 and 1947.

To a reader today, those words—Jews, 1940s, Poland—may not suggest anything particular. But to someone who lived through those years, the words evoke shudders of horror. For during that era, Adolf Hitler and his Nazi Party were rising to power in Europe. As Blima herself says, "[The Nazis] had some plan they talked about in these smoke-filled clubs, a plan for the country, the world. A plan which did not include Jews."

In order to understand the nightmare that overtook Blima and her family, some background information is helpful.

In 1936, when the story opens, much of Europe was in the grips of an economic depression. Millions of people were out of work. In Germany, conditions were particularly harsh. The country had been on the losing side of World War I, and it was broke from waging war. To make matters worse, the treaty that ended the war demanded that Germany pay some of the Allies (the countries that had fought against Germany, including Britain, France, the United States, and Russia) large sums of money to compensate for the suffering the war had caused. In addition, the treaty forbade Germany from establishing another army. All of these elements came together to make the German people feel bitter and hopeless. Humiliated, hungry, angry at the world and uncertain of the future, they looked for a leader—and someone to blame for their troubles.

As a result, when Adolf Hitler began talking about his plan to restore Germany's pride and prosperity, people were ready to listen. And when he suggested that the Jews were responsible for many of Europe's problems, his audience was happy to have a target for their anger and frustration.

Why did Hitler blame the Jews for Germany's problems? He was tapping into a vein of anti-Semitism (meaning "hatred of Jews") that had existed in Europe for centuries. Anti-Semitism was (and unfortunately, still is) both a form of prejudice and an expression of resentment and even jealousy.

Over the years, in part because of anti-Semitism, many European Jews had chosen to live in communities with other Jews, where they could practice their religion and customs together. Some of the Jews dressed differently than other Europeans; they observed Old Testament dietary rules called "keeping kosher"; they spoke Yiddish (a language related to German but including words from Hebrew and other languages). All these things led to bitter accusations against the Jews—that they were "clannish" and considered themselves superior to the *goyim*, or non-Jews, or that they were practicing secret rituals and even witchcraft. Anti-Semites also liked to remind people that, according to some interpretations of the New Testament, Jewish leaders participated in condemning Jesus to death. Calling Jews "Christ-killers" added fuel to the fires.

Jews were also resented because of the perception that they were financially better-off than many other Europeans. In general, this was a false perception—most Jews were just as impoverished as their neighbors. But because the Jewish culture had always emphasized learning and education, a number of Jewish people had become prominent in business and the professions. Anti-Semites encouraged their followers to believe that the "greedy Jews" were somehow responsible for their own poverty.

So this tradition of anti-Semitism was a handy one for Hitler to exploit for his own benefit. The Nazi philosophy was based largely on the idea of Germans being a "master race." "Germany above all" and "Germany for the Germans" were the Nazis' rallying cries. Hitler promised his listeners that he would make Germany "racially pure," thus restoring it to greatness.

In order to make his promises reality, Hitler developed a systematic plan to persecute the Jews. Nazis attacked Jewish businesses, breaking their windows and humiliating their owners. Jewish communities were sealed off and Jews were forbidden to leave. (The sealed communities were called "ghettos," a word that has entered our American vocabulary.) Jews were forced to wear a yellow six-pointed star—the Star of David—to publicly identify them.

In 1941, Hitler's top associates introduced what they called the "Final Solution of the Jewish Problem"—what we now know as the Holocaust. The solution was simply, and horribly, this: all of Europe's Jews would be exterminated. It was to help bring about the "Final

Solution" that Blima Weisstuch, age 25, was snatched on a spring day from the street in front of her parents' house.

Many Jews were transported directly to death camps, where they were murdered by being gassed or shot. Others, like Blima, went to work camps, where they were used as slave labor until they died of starvation, disease, or exhaustion. Some met an even more hideous fate. They were chosen as subjects in the Nazis' medical experiments, in which Nazi doctors tested the human endurance for such things as being frozen, poisoned, or operated upon without anesthesia.

Jews were not the only victims of the Holocaust. Gypsies, gay men, Jehovah's Witnesses, the mentally ill, the retarded, and other people the Nazis considered "inferior" were also sent to the concentration camps, where millions died or were killed outright. No one knows for sure how many people died in the Holocaust. Generally accepted estimates, however, are these: 6 million Jews, 3 million non-Jewish Poles, up to 800,000 Gypsies, up to 300,000 disabled people, about 25,000 gay men, and 2,000 Jehovah's Witnesses.

As the Allied armies defeated Germany throughout 1944 and 1945, they liberated concentration camps across Europe. Tragically, many of the prisoners found there were too weakened by disease and hunger to survive, and many thousands died in the weeks after liberation. Bergen-Belsen, Auschwitz, Buchenwald, and Dachau were some of the most infamous of the camps; you will find their names in Blima's story.

So there in a very small nutshell is a story of the what, where, and when of the Holocaust. What has not been addressed here is the biggest question of all: *How?* Whatever excuses were made, how could an entire nation accept the idea that millions of their fellow human beings—people who were simply going about their ordinary lives—should be rounded up and slaughtered as if they were rabid dogs?

One small bright light in the midst of all this horror is that fact that *not* all Germans (or people in other Nazi-occupied countries) turned their backs on their victimized neighbors. In Blima's story you will meet Gizella, a kind-hearted Catholic who helped her in the labor camp, despite great personal risk. You will also read of a Christian family who hid two young Jewish girls in their home for the duration of the war. There were thousands of non-Jews—their numbers are unknown—who risked their lives to hide Jews, help them, and even smuggle them out of Germany.

Still, the hideous fact is that the majority of Germans, as well as Nazi collaborators in other European countries, did *not* raise a hand to stop what was happening. After the war, many said that they were not aware of the horrors occurring within the concentration camps. It may be true that ordinary citizens did not know the exact details of what was happening. But as one looks back at the historical evidence, it seems clear that people did not know because they did not want to know. Jews and other persecuted people were disappearing in large numbers; the camps were highly visible; and Nazi leaders had publicly promised, again and again, to rid Europe of its "Jewish problem." It did not take a great deal of imagination to figure out what was going on in places like Dachau and Auschwitz.

Which brings us back to the question: How could such a thing happen?

Millions of words have been written trying to explain the grotesque slaughter that was the Holocaust. After sorting out all the history, excuses, and theories, one thing seems clear: Human beings are capable of incredible cruelty to one another once we manage to deny our common humanity.

When I stop thinking of my neighbor as "Alan" and begin thinking of him as "a Jew," or "a Muslim," or "a foreigner" or "a member of another race," it is easier for me to be unkind to him. From there, it's not such a big step to think of him as a thing, not a person—a sort of subhuman who does not feel love and friendship, who does not experience hope and despair, who does not deserve to dream and plan and live in peace the same way I do. And then, if he and his family vanish one night, it's not so hard to think, "It's not my problem. It's not as though it happened to people like me."

And that is the great value of a story like *The Story of Blima: A Holocaust Survivor.* Sometimes, the enormous nature of a catastrophe is too much to comprehend. Who can really grasp the idea of the murders of 6 million Jews? But in this story of one young Jewish woman, Blima Weisstuch—a daughter, a sister, a friend; a woman with the hopes and dreams common to all humanity—a reader can experience the reality of one of history's greatest tragedies.

PART I

BEFORE THE STORM

Chapter 1

"My name is Blima," I tell the young girl at the counter, handing her a box of fine round rolls; "it means 'flowers.'" The girl says nothing but quietly reaches up, holds the box of rolls against her chest for a moment, and skips off, her long braids bouncing behind her.

I love talking to the children who come into the bakery each afternoon when school is done. Their coat pockets holding coins from their parents, they walk proudly into the shop and look over each row of baked goods. There are long tan sourdough breads dripping flour like snowflakes, dozens of cookies winking at them with chocolate and prune eyes, and fat jelly doughnuts puffing red bubbles through their centers. Then each child makes a great show of deciding and points at the showcase. Sometimes, if I am lucky, they talk to me. These boys and girls are *goyim*— Christian children, not Jews like us. They are curious about the short, dark-haired Jewess behind the counter. They ask why the bakery is closed on Saturdays, what the narrow peg by the door (what we called the *mezuzah*) means, and why my head isn't covered by a scarf, like so many of the women they see. I, in turn, ask about the way they worship, why their Jesus is considered a savior, and what foods they give up for Lent—questions I would never dare ask their parents. The children answer generously. And in this way, we learn from each other.

It does not make me proud to say that this is the closest I have come to an education. Here in Poland in the year 1936, I left school after the eighth grade. I am now 20, and most girls my age, younger even, are already promised in marriage, and some even have one or two children. Although I too have a boyfriend, I am too busy at the shop to fill my head with thoughts of marriage. Aunt Rachel makes sure to remind me of that each morning just before she slides the last of the steamy baked goods onto the shelf and goes into the back room for her nap. Not many other young people could have put up with her as well as I do. I guess that's why Mama has chosen me, instead of my sisters, to work for her.

I don't much care for the way Aunt Rachel shakes her toothpick at me when she is making a point. Worst of all, she won't let me have any of the wonderful poppy seed muffins we sell because of a shortage of poppy seeds in our Polish city, Dombrowa. So I grow accustomed to eating the black bread, which isn't so bad even without butter, even if it is one or two days old and the moldy parts have to be cut away.

Aunt Rachel isn't really so bad, either. After all, she does let me eat the coffee cake crumbs that stick to the counter at the end of the day, and she does teach me how to make the proper change, and to tie a neat sailor's knot to close the white bakery boxes. Besides, she is my mother's sister, so what can I do?

I stand on my tiptoes and peer through the window at the far end of the shop. With the day nearing an end, half of a sun blinks like a golden eye behind the mask of a gray cloud. It is as if God Himself is coloring all of Dombrowa a melancholy purple. Soon the street lights will shine on each corner, and mothers will be hurrying their children to the table, while young couples giggle and whisper as they walk to dance halls in town. I quickly untie my apron and place one thick piece of black bread in a bag, along with an end piece for Masha, our family cat. As I am putting on my coat, the bells on the glass door sound, signaling my sister Adele's arrival.

"Blumke!" my sister exclaims, using my pet name. "So I am waiting outside and going to freeze from the cold already. Let's go!" I button my coat and say good-bye to Aunt Rachel, who glances up from her newspaper. Pointing her toothpick at me, she reminds me to lock the door.

When my sister Adele and I walk down the street, I think we look like two princesses. Certainly, I never feel that way alone. In fact, I most often want to sneak into the corners of my house and observe everyone's comings and goings like a quiet bird. But when I am with Adele, my favorite sister, her magical presence spreads to me. At these moments I feel, if not superior, at least as if I am some-body. I try to keep step with my sister's long strides as I rush alongside her. She shakes her head and laughs.

"I tell you, Blumke, you are slow, slow, slow!" she scolds.

I scowl in protest. "So who works as hard

as I do in this family?" I say. "You certainly do not."

"Well, of course, you were always the *best* child," she replies, giving me a sidelong glance and laughing again. But I can never be upset with Adele for long. She is simply too endearing, too beautiful. My affection for my younger sister covers any envy that might be in my heart.

I glance at her lovely round face. Even without her powder and cherry rouge, Adele is stunning. She has piercing chestnut-brown eyes, not pale blue ones like my own, and hers are shadowed by long, dark lashes. Her nose is a little upturned dot, not bold and prominent like mine and that of many other Jews. The mouth is embraced by full jewel-red lips which seem always parted in laughter. And her skin has an ivory sheen which glows free of any imperfection. Small wonder that last year she won first place in the local beauty contest.

We cross the wide road quickly, careful to avoid the cars that carelessly zoom down the street. Sometimes young men stick their heads out the window and whistle or shout suggestive remarks at us as we hurry along in our matching long brown coats with lamb collars.

"They always think we are twins," said Adele, kicking her long-booted legs higher as a wolf whistle sounds behind us. I snuggle my chin deeper into the warmth of my collar. How much I wish I were a twin to Adele. But no, the fates had not been so kind. My brother Froyim is my twin. Even under my heavy coat, I feel goosebumps rising up my arm, just thinking of him. Froyim—the yellow-haired lizard who was a head taller than I even at birth. Of all my brothers, it is he who looks most like our father. I suppose he thinks that gives him the authority to lord it over us all, and me especially. I constantly hear, "Blima, where are you going?" "Blima, don't be out too late." "Blima, watch out for the boys, they are all snakes, you know!" Wherever I go, it seems as if Froyim is walking in my shadow.

"Did you hear that one, Blumke?" Adele's musical voice shakes me out of my daydreams.

"Hear what?"

"Why, that tall boy over there, the one with the checkered cap," she says, pointing her chin slyly toward the left.

"Do you think I care what that boy was saying, or what any of them say, for that matter? Adele, remember that we are respectable girls. At least I know that I am."

"Oh, we all know how good you are, Blumke. And if we forget, we have Mama to remind us. Blumke is the *best* child!" she mocks, but her chestnut eyes twinkle merrily, without a hint of malice. Before I can protest, she continues, "But tell me, are you so good, so respectable with your friend Smulke?"

I can feel the heat of a blush rising up my cheeks.

"Of course I am. You know very well that—" but before I can finish speaking, Adele removes one delicate hand from her fur muff and boldly places it on my bosom.

"Why, you are!" she howls as she gives each breast a firm pat. "You are still binding them!" Again, I can feel the heat rising, this time up to my earlobes. I bite my lower lip to stop myself from crying.

"Really, Blumke, you would think that you are a Chinese woman in the nineteenth century. Only instead of binding your feet to keep your femininity, you are binding down your breasts to look like a man. This is Poland, and it is 1936, Blumke! 1936! Tell me, how do you tie them, with Aunt Rachel's baker's cord?"

I swallow hard before I can answer. Only Mama and my sisters know of this embarrassing action, which I began four years ago when

I turned sixteen. None of them understand how it feels to stand only four feet nine and have heavy breasts that point out half a foot as if to shout, "Here we are!" They don't know what it is to feel the eyes of men crawl over your chest. Nor can they guess what it feels like to squirm uncomfortably as male friends, cousins, even strangers reach out boldly to glide fingers over my breast as if it were one of the loaves of bread displayed in Aunt Rachel's shop.

"Never mind why I do it, Adele," I say, as I feel the warmth in my face slowly fade. "You just be glad that you don't have such problems. Besides," I add, grabbing her arm as we cross another busy street, "your mind shouldn't be on me or men, or anything but helping baby-sit our nieces tonight."

"Ah, yes, Blumke, you are so right," she says with a smile. "You are always so right, and always so *good*."

I sigh. If Adele only knew the times—the many times—when I wished I hadn't been quite so good.

Chapter 2

My brother Zalman was only two months old when he died. To be truthful, I hardly even remember what he looked like. Straight brown hair over a round, reddish face, like any baby. I don't even remember why Mama placed him in my arms one day. I do know that I was only a child myself, no more than six. I suppose he squirmed a little in my arms, as babies do, and I became afraid, and so I dropped him. It didn't take long for Zalman to die once his head hit the concrete at the bottom of the stairs. No one ever blamed me for it, though, not even Mama. After all, I was only a child myself.

Adele and I finally catch sight of the steep hill leading to our brother Victor's house. It is still snowing, and we know there will be hidden patches of ice the closer we get, so we steady ourselves against each other and dig in. It is already dark, and our figures in the snow cast long shadows as we approach.

Upon our arrival, Adele and I catch the tempting aroma of our sister-in-law Ruschia's chicken soup. By the time we reach the front steps, our two- and five-year-old nieces are already running toward us. Both little girls jump on me, demanding to know what I have brought them from the bakery. I reach into my coat and bring out a brown package Aunt Rachel gave me earlier. Inside are four minia-ture cakes, which the children quickly grab and stuff into their mouths. "Thanks, Aunt Blima, thanks!" they squeak.

Then Victor, my oldest brother, appears. "You are more than half an hour late," scolds Victor, as he gives each of us a quick kiss and hug. He and his wife are already getting into heavy lamb-lined coats as they prepare to go out for the evening.

Victor's round belly proclaims his love of both food and life. Straight out, like a woman five months pregnant! I often envy my nieces having Victor as a father, for his generosity, high spirits, and good nature help make his home a happy one. And Victor has been rewarded with an abundance of fortune. People say that he was born with a gold spoon in his mouth, but that is probably just their way of denying his genius for business. As a boy, Victor took a job pouring ten-pound bags of coffee and tobacco into smaller metal cans. Then he quickly worked his way up to assistant manager of that business. He now owns a small china store.

Ruschia holds her daughters' sugary fin-gers under a running faucet.

"Of course, you must finish your soup and chicken," she murmurs, "but how can you, now that you've eaten your dessert?" She plants a firm kiss on each child's forehead, reminding us where to find the plates and silverware.

Once my brother and sister-in-law have gone, Adele sets the table as I ladle the steaming soup into brown earthen bowls. The rich, sweet broth is wonderfully hot on a winter's evening. Once more, I remind myself to ask Ruschia for her recipe. Her soup, I have to admit, is better even than Mama's.

After a dinner of chicken, new potatoes, and corn, we bathe our little nieces and put them into their bed. The evening frost is strong enough to chill the blood, so Adele reaches up to the top shelf of the linen closet and pulls out a heavy white quilt. She spreads it over the girls and tucks it into the sides of the mattress. As I gaze at the smiling faces of my nieces, I wonder which of the two is prettier. Of course, the question is silly, for each is beautiful in her own way. Then I remember something Mama often said when we children would pester her to name her favorite. Holding up one hand in front of us, she would ask, "Which finger is most important to me, and which can I do without?" Of course, we couldn't answer, and so she would shoo us away, calling us "sillies" as she turned to her ironing.

As I kiss each of my nieces goodnight, my heart yearns for a daughter of my own. But I would never cut off her hair, as my sister-in-law has done with her daughters. No, my daughter will have long hair all the way down to her shoulders, just like a girl. A very feminine girl.

Chapter 3

I have been holding the words in for so long, that finally, almost as if by a will of their own, they have to come out.

"I'm not pretty, Mama!"

She glances over her shoulder at me, holding the cotton rag midair. "*Narishkeit*, such foolishness," she says under her breath, and continues rubbing the dusty wall mirror.

I am supposed to be helping, but there I am sitting in the yellow armchair by the window, my face pressed against a small hand mirror. It isn't like me to be so self-centered.

"Who says this, who?" my mother demands.

"Everyone notices Adele, the beauty queen."

Mama lets the cloth drop momentarily at her side and casts me a look of disappointment. "But, Blimala, you are—"

"I know, Mama, so good! Always the good one!" I lay the small mirror carefully on the dresser, run my finger around the border of tiny pink flowers, and scowl.

"Mirrors tell the truth, Mama," I whisper, and without my knowing, let fall a single tear. But already I know I have begun to test her patience. The idea enters my mind that she will fling the dirty rag at me in a fit of temper. Instead, she comes over and sits on the arm of the chair at my side. She picks up the hand mirror and places it so that both our faces are held in a single reflection.

"Do you see?" she says, staring into the glass. "Now, who is the pretty one?" A familiar vise gripped at my heart as the tears unleash.

"But . . . but of course, you are beautiful!"

"No, Blimala, it is you who are the most beautiful of all. See? See your eyes, their own blue, like your father's. Like the lake, when you were children, do you remember?" I bite my lip trying to recall the soft shimmer of the lake at the home of my cousins. We often played there in summers, the lake reflecting the blue tint of a sunlit sky.

"And the nose?" she continues.

"Oh, no, it is too big! Too big!" I squeal, cupping it with my hand.

"No, not big, but proud and dignified. There is no shame in it," she says, removing my hand.

"See the mouth?"

"Too small, thin-lipped like an old grandma!" At this she laughs.

"A grandmother? Oh, Blimala, here again

you are mistaken. Your lips are sweet and delicate and truthful. And yes, much like my own."

"And the freckles? Can they be removed, Mama?"

"Freckles? Spurts of sunshine, that is all." She sighs, and I feel her eyes move away from the mirror and glide slowly across my face. "Don't you see how much we look alike? Only you are much, much prettier. You are the best of me. And if that is not pretty enough, then what am I to say?" She places a soft arm around my hunched shoulders.

"Besides, what is pretty, anyway?" she continues. "Eyes? What does the color matter, as long as the ones you love can see themselves shining there? A mouth? Wide or narrow, so long as it speaks the truth. And the truth is that you, of all my children, are most like me. In looks, perhaps. But more importantly, here," she says, stroking the back of her hand across my forehead, "and here," placing it now against my heart.

"These are the places where we are most alike." She hugs me then, and resting in her arms, I never want her to let go.

Using the back of the armchair for leverage, she gets up abruptly, grabs the old rag, and proceeds to clean the bedroom dresser. I arise, place the small mirror aside, and take hold of the broom handle. It takes the two of us most of that afternoon to clean the rest of the house.

I don't recall ever discussing the way I looked with her or anyone after that. And in a few more months, I wouldn't even care.

Chapter 4

I remember the morning when I woke up and somehow sensed that my grandfather, Zayde, was going to die that day.

I dressed quietly so as not to wake my sisters. As I slipped on a nylon stocking, our Persian cat Masha came over to sniff at my toes. After securing my stockings to garters, I bend down to pet the Persian. She is growing too heavy for her own good. She mews softly under my touch, then curls her round body and bushy golden tail between my ankles. I lift her up, kiss her cold black nose, and smile as she tries to regain her balance on the waxed wooden floor.

As I brush the yellow strands off my stockings, I watch Masha's tail slip out the door as she heads toward Zayde's room. In a few minutes she will be lying next to his big feet, and her mewing will begin again. It is odd, considering Zayde has never shown anything but distaste for our cat, and Masha has always responded by carefully slipping out of sight at the sound of his sharp cane against the plank boards.

Mama always said cats and other animals have a sense of trouble coming: dogs pace before earthquakes occur, birds flutter as skies darken before a storm, and cats howl like frightened children before disaster. Perhaps that is why Masha has been sleeping at Zayde's feet the past few nights.

I am no more than half a block away from Aunt Rachel's bakery when the sense of dread I have been feeling suddenly grows larger. It's obvious something is wrong, for a small congregation of shopkeepers, some still wearing their aprons, has gathered in the middle of the gutter. I am not yet within hearing distance, but I can see some pulling at their beards, others gesturing wildly. And there is something else. As I draw nearer, I realize that a yellow scroll is plastered crookedly to the outside of each shop window. "JUDEN," it says, big bold black letters on yellow background. The sign means, "This shop is owned by Jews."

I push through the knot of storeowners and turn left toward the bakery. Underneath the shameless sign sits Aunt Rachel, looking round and small like a two-day-old roll. She clutches a soggy flowered handkerchief in one hand.

"What is it, Aunt? Why are all the people so angry? What is the meaning of these signs?" I ask.

Aunt Rachel spreads her palms before her and stares down at them as if she could find the answers in their lines. It is a few minutes before she speaks.

"Hitler's Nazis," she says, still gazing down. "It had to be. Didn't the fish seller across the street predict this? First one town, then another, and finally Dombrowa. It was only a matter of time."

I sit down on the bench next to my aunt, or rather slump suddenly, shocked by her words. Nazis. I had heard the name, even seen them once or twice zooming by in little black cars like bothersome insects. My brother Froyim had warned me of them. He had heard stories of assault, thievery, even kidnappings by this group. They meet in dark clubs where they salute each other and vow allegiance to a noisy little man, a painter by trade, named Hitler. His power has grown steadily in the last few months. These men, my brother warned, these Hitlerites, could be dangerous. They had some plan they talked about in their smoke-filled clubs, a plan for the country, the world. A plan that did not include Jews.

"Lower your head if you see one of them walking toward you and looking at you," Froyim had told me just the other day, "and if he begins to smile, run as fast as you can."

Of course, I ignored my brother's dire warnings, as I had all his other worries about my welfare. After all, I was not a political person like my younger sister Brandl. Although she was only twelve, Brandl had once pushed herself between two soldiers in order to snap a picture of Hitler saluting in that peculiar way from the top of one of those insect vehicles. Froyim and Brandl could have their speeches, their meetings, their protests. I just wanted to live my life.

But this is different. The Nazis are no longer part of some fairy tale, no longer confined to underground clubs, to angry words whose power fades as soon as breath touches air. They are in my world now, on the window of the bakery.

After about an hour of listening to the curses and laments of the other shopkeepers, Aunt Rachel places her hand on mine.

"Go home now, Blimala. The *goyim* will be too arrogant or too afraid to come in now. And the Jews, well, I don't think they will feel much like buying cookies today. Best to go home."

I nod and move as if to stand. But sitting next to Aunt, her light cotton jacket against the sleeve of my dark woolen coat, her rough hand atop my own small, rounded knuckles, I am unable to move further. And so we sit, for a long time, like two gray pebbles watching giant clouds roll across the darkening sky.

By the time I return home, my grandfather is dead. When I walk into his room, I see Mama's head buried against his feet, where our cat had lain only hours before. I can see the outline of Zayde's long, powerful body beneath the thick plaid blankets, looking as strong as I remembered. His head was hidden now by the thick fabric.

If it were possible for one human being to embody life's energy itself, that person would be my grandfather. In spite of the fact that he was a central figure throughout my life, I knew little of him. Yes, I knew he had a long beard as gray as steel coins. I knew that he was a rabbi once and later owned a shoe store, which he passed on to our father, and that he loved the taste of herring and onions. But beyond these things, I knew little, not even how he had become blind. Each evening until I started working for Aunt Rachel, I would hear the sound of his stick tapping against the concrete long before he reached the front door. As the oldest girl, it was my duty to make sure his glass of hot tea with lemon was set on the table before he entered, and I would have his woolen plaid blanket ready to drape over his knees after removing his heavy black boots. He rarely spoke to me. Occasionally, though, he would place his huge hand, with nails precisely trimmed by either Mama or myself, on my head, and murmur, *"Danke, shayna maydel."* Thank you, beautiful girl. A warm current would go through me then, for I knew that he never addressed my sisters, who were far prettier than I, in such a way. And even though I knew he was blind and saw me as no more than a shadow, if at all, I believed his words.

Like everyone else in the family, though, I also feared Zayde. Part of the reason was that we children didn't know him very well. But what we did know inspired awe. He had worked as a rabbi, a salesman, a train conductor, even a boxer, and survived the deaths of his wife of forty years as well as five children. He had lived with us for fifteen years, and spent all but the last year of his illness attending synagogue in the morning and helping my father, Tata, in the shop each afternoon. He was fairly silent at all other times, except on Saturdays, our day of worship. On those afternoons, he would gather my father, my brothers, and friends from the town around the metal kitchen table and regale them with stories from the Talmud, our holy book, between bites of Aunt's sponge and honey cakes. Sometimes, late at night, I would pass by his room and notice a soft light coming from within. With the intent of shutting the door, I would enter slowly to see his back rhythmically swaying, his head and shoulders covered by the faded blue and white prayer shawl. Once, and only once, I heard him cry out in the fervor of his prayer, "*Surala*," the name of his dead wife, my grandmother.

My mother looks up from the blanket, now soaked with her tears.

"Blimala!" she exclaims, reaching her arms toward me, "Zayde is dead!"

"I know, Mama, I know," I say, returning her warm embrace, letting her dampen my cheek and loosened hair with her kisses and tears. I take both her hands in mine, and not knowing what to say, add, "It is better for him now, Mama. He is at peace."

"Better for him, but not for me. Not for me, Blimala!" she cries, flinging herself across Zayde's motionless legs. I remain standing, waiting for Mama to look up, brush back the strands of my hair, or fix my collar. But she only lifts her head briefly, her eyes still fixed upon the blanket, and directs me to wash up and run down the block to the synagogue so that preparations can be made. Tomorrow there will be a burial.

I do not walk into the bathroom, though, but head straight for Mama's bedroom. This is my first real encounter with death, and I pull away from the thought of Zayde no longer coming home to pat my head or swaying in silent prayer. Most of all, though, I fear the change in Mama. I need her to make sense of it all, to tell me that yes, it will be all right today, tomorrow. So, instead of running to the synagogue, I quietly slip off my boots, turn down the covers, and find the indentation of Mama's body still in the sheets. Then, as I have done so many times before, I mold my body into that spot. And when I can smell the lilac of her hair, the peaches in her skin, I close my eyes and take a long deep breath.

Chapter 5

At my grandfather's funeral, I faint. As if in a dream, I feel myself falling in slow motion, head first into the open grave. A voice, my father's, I think, screams out. And then all is black.

When I awake, I find myself in an old wooden cart that minutes before had been used to transport Zayde. Mama is pressing smelling salts against my nose with one hand and stroking the top of my head with the other. A few feet away, I can hear my sisters arguing.

"Didn't I tell you not to let her stand there?"

"And could I force her to stand in the back? Don't be such a child!"

"Fine. So now we almost had two in the grave, because you can't watch anything but your own manicured fingernails!"

Abruptly, the argument ceases; no doubt my sisters catch sight of our Tata's stern eye. My father has only to turn his head, and he commands the will of an entire household. For Mama's part, she ignores the whole affair.

"Blimala, are you better?" I nod, assuring her that I am. Only when she sees the gradual return of color to my pale cheeks do we move off the cart into the bright sunshine. A strong breeze is blowing, and I pull my cotton kerchief tighter around my head. These fainting spells are more embarrassing than worrisome, and I hate the attention they bring me. I reassure them all that it was only a touch of an old anemia, made worse by the lack of a proper breakfast in the morning. Finally all but Mama turn back toward the gravesite and the men who are all now swaying in prayer. Mama keeps tight hold of my hand.

When we walk silently back to the row of cars, I am oddly thankful for the diversion my fainting spell has created. My mother's face is still marked with heavy tears, but for the moment she forgets her sorrow.

When we reach home, one of the neighbors is already there, and she comes running outside with a pitcher of cold water to pour over our hands. Except for the covered mirror and an eerie silence that has descended over the household like a shroud, it appears that all is ready for a party. Platters of herring, salmon, and vegetable salads line the dining table; huge whitefish lie in beds of dark green lettuce, the open eyes of the fish assuming a ghostly glare beneath the crystal chandelier. In the center stands a giant bowl of perhaps three dozen hard-boiled eggs, all peeled, naked, white, and cold to the touch.

Once inside, we are beckoned immediately to place them in our mouths. The circle of life must continue. I bite into the softness of the egg as I watch my mother, father, brothers, and sisters do the same, and I have a certain feeling of comfort. Grandfather is no longer with us; that is true. But here we all are eating eggs together just as we did almost every morning, in the same way that the sun would rise from the gray of dawn each day. Each day, no matter what. I wash down the yolk with a glass of sweet tea.

As the men go into the living room to pray, more neighbors slowly filter into the house to pay their respects. Each person stops in front of Mama and, as is the custom, says a prayer in order to comfort her. A group of women encircle her, encouraging her to eat and drink, for the sake of her children if not herself. And before long, I am even able to catch the hint of a smile wash across her face as she munches on a thick slice of buttered challah bread.

The children, as they are inclined to do, take the time as an opportunity to play hide-and-seek throughout the rooms, and eventually their laughter and squeals draw my father out of his prayers and into the kitchen.

Adjusting his eyes to the light, Tata turns his massive head until his vision falls on my youngest brother, Kalman.

"Is this a party, or what? Do you think this is a playtime for you and your friends?"

Kalman remains as if glued in the corner, pushing his chin against his chest. "No," he answers.

"No, what?"

"No, Tata. Not a party."

"Of course it is not a party. Remember, God sees all. You of all people should know that."

"Yes, Tata. I'm sorry, Tata."

When Tata has left the room, Mama turns her head to the frowning child, beckoning him with one finger. Immediately, he runs to her, and wrapping him in her arms, she kisses his brown eyes, which are glistening with tears. I watch as Kalman soaks up her love the way a roll takes in the full taste of gravy once dipped inside. As he rests his head on her lap, one can still see the baby he was, in spite of the fact that in just over a year he will celebrate his bar mitzvah, the ceremony marking a Jewish boy's passage into adulthood. Already he has begun to accompany Tata to the front pews of the synagogue. At those times, Mama smiles down at him from her place with us on the synagogue balcony, murmuring "Child, child."

I can't find my dress shoes. I have spent all morning looking for them, in the closets, under the sofa, behind the cartons of Passover dishes, even in Tata's wardrobe, where he hangs his prayer shawl. I have questioned my sisters, asked Mama if she has perhaps borrowed them or lent them to someone, all in vain. More than anything in the world, I hate losing things. I grow frantic, begin tossing scarves, books, trinkets into the middle of the floor. Beads of sweat falling like raindrops from my brow, I run from room to room, my eyes darting north, south, west, east, back to north again. I forget how to sit. I forget how to speak. I scream. In short, the search has made me a crazed person.

Mama comes running in. Laying her eyes on the chaos in front of her, her hands fly to her head.

"Blimala, what have you done?"

"My shoes, Mama. The new ones Tata gave me. The blue silk with the little white bow and the skinny heels. I can't find them. I've looked everywhere, and I can't find them at all!" I throw my hands up into the air and fall back into the bed, utterly desolate.

Mama shakes her head and gives me a sad look.

"Blima, I am surprised at you. Over shoes you go so crazy?" she says, stooping to pick up a pink striped scarf.

"But you know how I hate to lose things. And how I always, always have everything in its place."

"I know all that, many times I know it," Mama sighs, impatience creeping into her voice. "But I also know how smart you are. When you lose something, you must think and not go running and screaming. Just sit down calmly and think." She picks up a heavy dictionary from the corner of the room and hands it to me.

"Fine," I say, returning the book to its place on the shelf. "But they match the dress so nicely, and besides, Tata had to order them special, and—"

"And so? Tata can order again. You go to the store and look in the catalog, and he can order again. Besides, you will find the shoes before that. We are not looking for a needle here, but shoes. Blima, Blima, this is your worry? Better to worry about bigger things."

"Very well. You're right. They have to be here someplace," I answer, trying to restore a sense of calm to my voice. As I stoop to retrieve the rest of the shoes and skirts scattered on the floor, I think about the "bigger things" Mama says we have to worry about. Sickness. The family businesses. The Nazis in the streets. Neatly folding a kerchief and placing it on a closet shelf, I shut my mind to all that. I think it best to worry about the shoes instead.

That night, I turn slowly as Mama draws chalk lines across the bottom of my new dress. I still haven't found the shoes, but am wearing a pair of Adele's new spring ones that have the same type of heel. Mama hums Jewish melodies as she works.

"Mama, do you think this neckline makes my bust look too big?"

She looks up exasperated and just shakes her head. Satisfied, finally, she places her tape measure in an apron pocket and stands up. Wiping her hands on the apron, she brusquely pulls up the shoulders of the dress and gives the scalloped neckline a yank.

"Very nice," she murmurs to herself, then stoops down again with a bunch of pins in her mouth. Mama looks round and small, I think, as she labors at my knees. Her bust is full, her hips ample, and stretched over all is the whitest skin, untroubled by the brown sprinkles which I have inherited from God knows where. In character, though, we are alike; at least I hope so. We never walk, but run as if pursued by time. We rarely embrace, but when we do, it is with a spontaneous surge of emotion, like a waterfall. People sometimes say I look like her, but I don't think so. Her bright eyes dance under sparse brown brows, but they gleam brown, not a dull blue like my own. And they crinkle in the corners when she laughs, which is often. Her nose is strong and average, and her smile, though thin-lipped, is always full and genuine between cheeks that glow red without even a touch of rouge. Mama's hair, when not pushed beneath a scarf, falls straight chestnut and vibrant to her shoulders. Her maturity gives her an aura of beauty that none of her daughters, not even Adele, can touch. Of course, she doesn't realize it at all. She never even looks in a mirror.

My sister-in-law Ruschia walks over to assess my outfit. She circles me appraisingly.

"Pretty!" she exclaims, kissing the tips of her fingers. That makes me feel good. Ruschia always tells the truth.

"And the bust?" I ask, giving the neckline another yank.

"A little cleavage is good, too. At least you got," she laughs. Ruschia is sweet. No, she is more than that. She is wise, too. She, Victor, and the girls have formed a habit of visiting our home at least twice a week, so she has become as a sister to us. Well, actually, she has always been a part of the family, even before she married my brother. Ruschia is our second cousin, and when she and her sister lost their parents it was only natural that a marriage be arranged between Ruschia and the eldest cousin. Mama and Tata had to sign the permission certificate, as Ruschia was only fourteen. I am glad no one has arranged a marriage for me, although I secretly hope I can one day love Smulke, who is tall, blonde, and perfect, the way that Victor and Ruschia love each other.

"Let's hope your friend Helen will be married," Ruschia murmurs, almost to herself.

"What?"

"Your friend Helen and her gentleman. I hope they can have their wedding."

"What are you saying? Why would they not marry?" I ask, growing agitated.

"Well . . . look, Blimala, I do not mean to frighten you, but you know how it's been lately. In the streets, in the stores, and now they look, make faces, and laugh even when we go into the synagogue. And that Hitler—well, you can read the papers for what he says about us. It is just . . . just hard for us now; that's all I mean."

"Well, I just don't believe it is as bad as all that," I retort, moving uneasily until Mama, pins in her mouth, shoots me a cross look.

"You know about my friend Rifka and her beau, don't you?" Ruschia says. "The laughing and name-calling was bad enough, but when the two were exiting the synagogue for the first time as man and wife, one of those Nazi thugs snatched the groom's hat right off his head. Then another had the nerve to step on Rifka's train that her mother made with her own hands. I didn't see, but heard, that an egg flew at them from God knows where. Fortunately, it missed. I tell you, Blima, these are uncertain times now. Just so you know."

"So it is, Ruschia, but a name is just a name. And what is a hat or an egg? Should we stop our lives because of some idiots? Run to England, to America? This is not for me. I'm not ready to give up my life just yet." I look down at Mama, who rises from her work with a look I can't quite make out. Removing the pins from her mouth, she eyes her handiwork intently.

"Let's pray to God everything will be okay," Mama says.

From the armchair, Ruschia looks up at her mother-in-law, searching her face. "Mama," she asks, "*do* you think it will be okay? I mean, every day they taunt us more; every day they restrict us more. There are even rumors they are grabbing Jews from the streets. Do you really think it will be okay?"

Mama smiles at her lovingly. "I believe in God. I have to believe," she answers.

Mama helps me down from the platform I stand upon. Suddenly, we are shocked upright as a high-pitched whine shoots through the air. It takes only seconds for us to realize what it is, and we run into the kitchen. There, golden-haired Masha lies coiled on the windowsill. Between screeches she is furiously licking the frost off the window. She has taken to making these awful noises lately, sometimes at dawn or just as the darkness descends, and no one can quite figure it out. She had left Zayde's bed soon after his death and spends most of her days at one window or another, sending up these desperate whines. Not whines—cries, really. They sound much like human cries.

It is useless to tempt her with food, even her adored tuna, and she only yowls louder if we try to get her to go outdoors. Realizing it is useless, we try to ignore her. Eventually, she stops.

My feet have begun to hurt in Adele's shoes. I hurry toward the bedroom to remove them along with the dress so Mama can begin the sewing, but just before I turn into the hallway, I am stopped by something. In the parlor sits my father in a high-backed upholstered chair. He is reading the paper and frowning beneath small gold-wired spectacles; the curls of his black beard brush the page. On the floor to his left are my younger brother and sister, stretched out to play a game of checkers. Sitting on the couch with a big bowl of purple grapes between them are my older brothers, arguing as usual over a point of business. Victor, always easy-going, laughs as Froyim jumps up with wild gestures and bends toward his brother in an attempt to use his height to enforce a point. Underneath a giant window with emerald green drapes is Adele. She has just learned to knit, and is lost in concentration over a stitch in a winter sweater that she is creating. Over all, above Tata's chair, a portrait of his great-grandfather, dressed in black with beard down to the waist, surveys us all somberly.

"Blimala," Tata motions to me, "turn on the light." The lamp, one of three in the room, is covered by a stained-glass shade decorated with apricots and oranges. Switched on, it casts a stream of pale yellow light into the room. For a moment I feel myself suspended in its ray. I float, led by the light, into the room where the others, my family, form this classic scene. How neat, I think, how ordered my life is. Everything is in place as it should be. I let the light seep into my brain, circle and warm it. When I turn toward the bedroom, the dots of light dance before me.

I take off the dress, hang it on a padded hanger, and sit down on the bed. Masha pads quietly in, mewing softly. I pick the cat up and stroke her slowly on my lap. My eyes carefully taking in each corner of the room, I resign myself to the loss of the shoes.

PART II

DARKNESS FALLS

Chapter 1

It is a spring day when I see my mother for the last time. I am returning home early from Aunt Rachel's bakery. It has been another day in which business is so poor it doesn't even make sense to run the ovens and turn on the lights. Wishing not to let the goods go to waste, Aunt sends me home with armfuls of brown rolls and still-warm loaves of raisin bread. I can smell the full raisin-scented sweetness as it mingles with the fragrance of newly cut grass. It is the first day when one can say with certainty that the new season has arrived, after months of biting cold and sidewalks coated with ice. How I long to remove my old blue woolen coat, but I can't both carry it and keep the breads intact. Besides, I can already see the concrete stoop and little patch of grass which signal home. I quicken my pace.

From here, everything goes fuzzy. I think I hear bootlike footsteps from behind. I think I feel someone's breath sliding down my neck like a black veil. I think I see a flash, a car, and I become aware that my arms and legs are no longer mine. I am lifted up and away by a will stronger than mine. Out of the corner of my eye I see Mama. She is on the stoop in her blue apron, her hair wrapped with a white cotton kerchief. Then her hands fly to her head and out into the stiff air. "*BLIMA!*" she screams. She is running toward me. "*BLIMA!*" But I have been picked up, and I'm flying through the air against my will. My senses go numb as the Gestapo, the Nazi secret police, push me into the wagon where others wait with bowed heads. "*BLIMA!*" I hear my mother call, "*BLIMA!*" But then her voice fades, and the nightmare begins.

Chapter 2

I am walking in the snow. The girl in front of me falls, and I bend to pick her up, linking my arm through hers. "Hurry!" someone shouts, and we quicken our pace. Although I can no longer feel my hands, I push a strand of hair off of my eyes. I walk.

The sun pierces a path of bright yellow through the forest, and we follow it. It must be past noon now, for I can see the remnants of the heavy winter snow have begun to melt, leaving circles around emerging twigs. Some of the girls have begun bending and quickly plucking the twigs, hoping the soliders will not notice. They push the bits of green into their mouths, then munch slowly, eyes on the yellow path. They never miss a step. I forget the round white potatoes and warm stew from my mother's table, and think only of my empty yearning stomach and how delicious those green buds look.

"You," I whisper to the girl whose arm is linked in mine, "I will get us some of those twigs right there. Do you think you can walk alone for a moment?" She lets her head fall in a nod of sorts, then opens her mouth to speak, but only a dry cough comes out. She looks me full in the face, and I see she is a girl of no more than sixteen or seventeen. I slowly disentangle my arm from hers, keeping up the steady march. When I see her steps are in line with the rest, I lower myself and allow my arm to brush across a patch of fledgling twigs, like a swooping bird, and gather them into my hand. I link my arm in the girl's again and press a few of the twigs into her hand.

"Eat," I whisper. And the two of us consume our precious snack, tough and covered in dirt, as if it were a slice of honey cake.

Somewhere, a shot rings out. It is the third time we have heard the sound since beginning our march. But already we have learned not to stiffen or cry out. When an older woman had cried out at the sudden gunfire, we witnessed the butt of a rifle slapped across her back. So instead, we let our disbelief and fear pass silently through our bodies as we keep walking.

It is dark now, and, forgetting the nightmare I am in for a moment, I look next to me so that I can link my arm through my sister Adele's for warmth. Hanging onto my elbow instead is the exhausted girl beside me. I am tired too, but I know I must keep walking.

I remember what happened when I was

seized yesterday. It seemed like hours that I sat next to a soldier to my left and a girl, a phantom at first, to my right. Remembering my brother's warning, I kept my eyes riveted to the floor of the car, strewn with pieces of tissue and cigarette butts. As the cold metal of the soldier's black Lugar pistol pressed against my hip, I was grateful that I still wore the coat that covered my body. I swallowed the wad of saliva stuck in my throat, and tried not to think when the ride ended and we found ourselves at a waiting train.

"Get in!" the commandant ordered, and we quickly climbed up into one of the cars. It was like a cattle car, really, full of frightened figures, all girls and women, huddled in each corner. They were girls once adored by parents who tucked them securely into bed each night. They were women once flattered by men who stepped aside when they entered a room. But now, each one of us was only a Jew. And that, we would soon find out, meant we were less than animals.

When enough of us had filled the space that, I think, it could hold no more, we heard the last "Get back there!" and the last "Faster!" The door creaked abruptly shut.

I was clinging to a protruding wooden beam in one corner, praying I would not faint, when I heard my name called.

"Blima? Blima Weisstuch, is that you?" I turned to the mass of women in front of me, but was unable to find the source of the meek voice.

"Blima . . . Straight in front. It is me, Clara. We were schoolmates. In Mrs. Linbraum's class?" I saw an arm emerge from the crowd, and I grasped it firmly, pulling it toward me.

"Clara. Do you know me? Clara Reitman from Dombrowa," she repeated, a hint of a smile flickering across her face. I looked into her eyes and recognized the phantom who had been sitting next to me on the ride to the station.

"Clara? Why, I—"

"I knew you did not recognize me with the hair," she said, reaching up to touch a crown of blonde curls. "Colored it last year, you know. And the baby fat, well, that is gone now too!" she added, patting her flattened stomach. "You, though, Blima, look exactly the same as when we sat next to each other in the seventh year class. It *is* good to see you!"

She inclined her head toward mine and whispered, "I noticed you right away when they pulled you in, but I didn't dare say anything. You know . . . the guns."

I nodded. It was good to see an old

friend from home, and I clasped her to me like a sister.

"Do you have any idea where they are taking us?" she whispered.

I shook my head as I bit into my lip, regretting every time I closed my ears to the warnings to watch out for Nazi soldiers. Clara touched my hand. "Don't fret over it. They would have taken us no matter what."

Had she heard of others, like ourselves, being captured? But Clara, it seemed, was as blind as I had been.

"No one I know. And certainly no one from Dombrowa." But she had heard stories of girls grabbed off the streets elsewhere, as we had been, or from inside shops, schools, even hospitals.

After one hour, or perhaps two, the train screeched to a halt, and those sitting against the walls of the car felt their bodies and hearts move upward as all eyes stared at the door.

"Quickly! Move faster!" The barks reached our ears even before the door ground open. Hopes of an arrival at a destination, wherever that might have been, or better yet, a rest stop, were dashed as another twenty or so women were pushed into our car.

"Where do we go now? There is no more room!" came the desperate cry from the rear.

A Nazi hoisted himself on board like an ominous beetle.

"*Vas?*" he demanded, brandishing a silver pistol. No one dared speak. He stood some minutes peering into the crowd as we squeezed tighter against each other. Although my German was poor, I understood enough to know his next words were a threat. The car, if we liked, could be made lighter by a few at this very moment. Then the horrifying realization came to me: *He is liking this.*

As he spoke, I forced myself to stare down, down, at the assembly of shoes before me. High buttoned. Brown. Leather boots. Alligator. Chunky wooden heels. Maroon with fur trim. Where had these shoes been headed before ending up here on the dirty straw-laden floor of a cattle car?

And then, a word.

"*Bitte, capitan...mine boach.*" Please, captain, my stomach. A black Lugar rose into the air and shivered briefly. An explosive sound pierced the car, and we women shrunk back as one. There was a scream from the speaker, who fell against some of the others in the back. The rest of us were silent.

I dared not look at the fallen woman, but kept my eyes to the ground. Some minutes later, I heard movement, a shuffling of feet, as

a few of the others propped her body in a corner. I glimpsed her shoes, high-buttoned, a
scuffed oxford brown. The German bellowed
an animalistic note of triumph next to me,
and I could feel his stinking breath against my
cheek.

Don't faint now, Blima, I thought to
myself. Blima, don't faint.

Chapter 3

Not knowing is perhaps the worst thing that can befall a person. To know a thing for certain, even if it is tragic, brings a sense of doneness, a sense of peace. But not knowing slithers into the heart like a silent snake, making every blood vessel quiver with anxiety. Today I know where I am. But tomorrow? Last week I was standing in my mother's kitchen peeling potatoes as she placed them into a pot of boiling water, one by one. Yesterday, the same hands were reaching out to me as I sped away in a car to the place where I am today. But where exactly is this place? And where is my mother? Will I know my way back to her? Is she even at home? Am I to be lost forever? Perhaps it is best not to think at all.

I have been walking since we left the train some hours ago; I don't know how many. My thoughts keep returning to the high-button brown oxfords, and even though I never knew their owner, I can feel the tears coming into my throat. I swallow them, for I know already the cost of crying. Instead, I focus on the icy land that seems to stretch without end ahead of me.

I have been separated from Clara, but I feel her presence somewhere in the forest behind me. I keep moving my feet and learn to forget the gnawing hunger pain in my belly. The twigs that have supplied us with nourishment have vanished. Every so often a woman falls. She is either shot or remains there on the ground. There is no child's hand to stroke her forehead, no comforting prayers for the family. My companion on this endless march was one of those who have fallen. So I ignore again the biting hunger that grips me now and then. I only know to move forward.

At last there is a clearing, and I hear a soundless sigh of relief, not for reaching who knows what, but for at last being able to stop. I see the sign as we rush through barbed wire with spotlights and guard dogs and Germans, guards on all sides. What are they afraid of? A group of women with weary bones and empty spirits? The sign says "Grunberg." It is as I thought. We are in a forced labor camp somewhere in Poland. The year is 1941, and I am a prisoner.

I stand in front of an unsmiling German woman commandant. Without a word, she peels the blue coat off my body as I hurriedly tug the watch off my wrist and pull on the simple gold chain on my neck until it breaks. I silently thank God that it is not summer, so the small diamond ring Smulke gave me last year slides easily off my finger. Those who are not so lucky must endure the barks of the soldiers as they pathetically struggle to remove a ring from a swollen finger. I toss these possessions onto a growing mountain of valuables. Next I am pushed along to a table where another female guard, also without a word, grasps my arm and tattoos a five-digit number on it. So now I am no longer Blima, but a number. Can it be that Hitler's plan for the towns to become *Judenrein*, free of Jews, has actually come to be?

But I have little time for speculation as I am pushed on again. My hair is shaved, my pink cashmere sweater and woolen plaid skirt changed for a white blouse and black skirt bigger than I by two sizes. Somewhere in all this I lose my shoes. On my feet are wooden soles with pieces of canvas stretched across, coverings more than real shoes, and also too big. I move on.

Finally, and it can only be thanks to God, we are placed in small bunks filled with straw. There are perhaps fifty of these in the barracks, and I find myself in a middle one. I glimpse a girl below, only a few years younger than I. She is hyperventilating, and when I see her arm extend, I reach out and encircle her wrist with my hand. She begins to cry silently. "Mama, where are you?" she whispers. I squeeze the wrist but have no strength to do more. We have all lost our mothers here.

It is black in the barracks except for the bright yellow beam that periodically shoots through the small windows and sprays the room with light. We sleep, but our dreams are restless and troubled. Always my mother is running after me, arms outstretched; always the Gestapo is pulling her back, pushing me forward. Her screams pierce the air and encircle me. "Blima!" she sobs, until I awake. Battling the sleep from my tired eyes, I still hear her. Yet it is no longer my mother's voice which calls my name, but another.

"Blima! Are you sleeping?"

I look up and see only another head covered with brown stubble bobbing above. But the voice is a familiar one.

"Clara? . . . Is that you?"

"Yes, Blima, I thought it was you I saw before, but I was too afraid to speak . . . What luck, no?"

I sigh with relief to be with someone I know.

"I slept as though I would never get up,"

Clara says. "But I am afraid to sleep, afraid to be awake. What time do you think it is now? Those bastards took the one gold watch I had from my girlhood. And then, of course"—her voice cracks here—"the hair . . . Why would they take our hair, Blima?"

"Lice, I think," I answer, touching my own shorn scalp. I peer through the window on my left only to view pitch blackness, and I think even hell has its fires. "Perhaps it is one or two in the morning; I don't know," I answer.

"They will wake us in a few hours as soon as one stream of light comes through the horizon, so we'd best get to sleep," Clara says.

"Clara?"

"Yes, Blima?"

"How do you know that? I mean, do you know what is to happen to us?"

I could feel shifting above as Clara moves to a sitting position.

"There are others here who know. Do you remember Sala and Annie from our school? I was walking with them in that damned forest. They have heard news of others in these camps. It is not so bad as long as you are willing to work. They told me, in fact, that they came voluntarily."

Voluntarily? This was not to be believed.

"No, Clara. How can that be? You saw with your own eyes what they did to that woman on the train. People dropping like flies on the ground . . ."

"I tell you, Blima, this will be a paradise compared to the uncertainty of staying home. Who knows what is in store for the others?"

I wasn't sure what Clara meant, but I didn't want to think about it then. "Clara, what do you mean we will be okay if we work? What kind of work?"

"Any kind. Digging ditches, washing out their pots of sauerbraten, whatever they demand. Remember, when they ask if you can do it, just say yes. Think of nothing else."

I hear Clara stretch out on the straw and know that I will soon hear the steady breathing of her sleep.

She spoke of not knowing what was to be back home. Not knowing. The not knowing can tear someone apart, Mama would say when Tata would arrive home late from the synagogue or my brother Kalman was kept an extra hour for scripture study. I turn in my bed, hoping to turn away too from the thoughts of home which plague me, now that I have stopped moving. It is then that I hear the soft crinkling sound from beneath my shirt, and I remember. Thrusting my hand between the binding and the brassiere, I pull out several photos. To think I had almost forgotten them! Weeks ago, having heard that the young people were being abducted from the streets, I grabbed my store of family photos and placed them each morning beneath the bindings across my chest, close to my heart. Just in case.

I look at them and know that I will look and look again each day that I remain here, however long that may be. Mama always said that when the memories fade, as they surely must, all we have are the pictures. And here they are, all with me again. One of me and my sisters. Another of my brother Victor and his wife Ruschia and their precious little daughters. There are also pictures of my other brothers, including my twin brother Froyim.

I also have the small photo taken by my sister of Hitler himself waving from a car. I search his face for some answer, but I see none, so I put it away. I feel my breathing coming easier now as I gaze over the photos. They are all here. All except Mama and Tata. They arranged to have pictures of their children, never themselves. No matter. Mama's face, they say, was stamped upon my own. And her spirit, I knew, had long been within my heart.

I return the photographs to their hiding place beneath my blouse and push my face into the straw. With the hours till daylight waning, there is but one thing I know for certain in this uncertain world. Tomorrow I must be prepared to work.

Chapter 4

Four a.m. A shrill whistle shocks us awake. We jump from our bunks and line up for roll call.

"Pinch your cheeks," someone whispers, and word goes down the line. We pinch until it hurts and pray that the look of health we had only days ago will return. When the woman commandant turns to inspect the others, we wait, shoulders back, standing tall. Looking at the girls opposite us, I know that we are a sorry bunch.

The commandant must be a man, I think, for I find no trace of femininity, no softness, in her long face. Her dark hair is cut short, and her body is tightly wrapped in a thick coat with gold buttons. In one hand she holds a whip; in the other there is a leash attached to a large German shepherd she calls Otto. A dog is given a name, I think, but we ourselves are but numbers. As the commandant walks down the line for inspection, I try to glimpse her eyes. But I am unable to tell their color. If there is such a hue as muddy steel, I decide, they are that. Certainly they hold no clue to a soul. When she walks past me, I look away.

She sits down with the dog beside her and

begins to call numbers. I have never memorized mine, and I quickly look down. 44703. The girl who has been assigned as our leader pulls out any girl who dawdles.

"44703!"

I jump forward as if by a spark and join the others. I don't know if hearing my number is a good or bad thing, but then our group of about 25 begins to march toward the main barracks where I can already smell the bean soup. When we enter, my hopes are born out. I am given a portion of bread and a cup of tasteless soup. The black bread is not like Aunt Rachel's, even on its eighth day. Yet I devour both it and the watery soup quickly as if they were manna from heaven. Only much later do I realize I must not rush so, for the food hits my stomach ferociously. I must learn to eat more slowly, not to savor it exactly, but to give my system a chance to digest properly. We go to the toilet, mere holes in the ground, and relieve ourselves. We are given ice water, which we pour quickly over ourselves, happy to feel refreshed. And then we march.

The sun, the same sun I would see from my room at home, rises full and proud over the mountains. The air has a crispness from the last traces of winter's frost, and as we march, I see the mountains, first a dusty blue, emerge from the clouds. As we draw closer, I see each hillock ringed by the promise of green, and I take comfort in the fact that the earth is still here. I try not to think of my swollen knees, the tiny pebbles beneath the wooden soles that attack me mercilessly with each step. The earth is still here, and so is the sun. Everything is the same, and for a moment I see myself walking up the steps to the home of my parents, coming to the door. My only worry is that it will be closed.

A girl in front of me trips on a stone, and the lash comes swiftly down. I see her standing up and marching again as if bothered only momentarily by a fly. The lady commandant in the heavy boots laughs and calls her a stupid cow.

We arrive at a factory where there are two women overseers. One is short, with sacks of ruddy flesh on her cheeks and under her chin. Her short, white hair is slicked back from her face, giving it the appearance of a tennis ball. She walks up and down the rows of girls with much effort, and when she stops in front of me, I notice a nervous tic in her right eye. She smiles, but it seems like an evil smile. She even tells us her name, Helga, and assures us, smiling again, of our good fortune in being chosen for this labor.

But it is the other overseer who inspires fear in me. She is tall, taller than any of the girls or the guards, for that matter. Unlike Frau Helga who wears a simple blouse and long skirt, Frau Gizella wears a jumper with huge pockets. The pockets seem to be full, and I can see what I believe to be a thick rope emerging from one of them. Her platinum blonde hair sits atop her head like a crown. From the moment I enter the factory, her blue eyes never leave my face.

"Can you sew?" She asks me the same question she has asked of each girl down the line.

I remember Clara's advice and swiftly reply, "Yes, Commandant." I have no clue how to sew even a sock, but I tell her I can. The ominous-looking black sewing machines wait, row by row, in the vast factory. If only I had watched Mama more carefully! If only I had paid attention. If only . . .

The girls who say they cannot sew are led out of the factory through what appears to be a long tunnel. The rest of us sit down, each at a machine piled with sturdy brown tweed uniforms, perhaps thirty in all. I lift the spool of thread and try to attach it to the bobbin. It slips from my hand and rolls to the floor, but no one notices as I quickly retrieve it.

One of the girls has been found out, and I watch as Frau Helga stomps quickly toward her and grabs her by the neck. The pity is she has no hair to be pulled.

"What is wrong with you?" Frau Helga cries, dragging her toward the door through which the others have disappeared. The girl, a skinny one of no more than sixteen, has learned and makes no sound as she proceeds down the long tunnel. When the doors have closed, Helga rubs her chubby hands together as if to cleanse them of some vermin.

"To work, to work," she snickers, eying each of us.

I return to the thread and bobbin, which I somehow master. I am trying to position a collar to be sewn at the neck of a uniform when suddenly I look forward and see two huge pockets before me.

Frau Gizella places large but surprisingly smooth hands on the machine, bends her head, and peers directly into my eyes. I remember the rope in her pocket, and for a moment my heart stops.

"Your name?" she asks. I recite my number.

Gizella closes her eyes and shakes her head slowly. The other girls have begun their work and take no notice.

"Your *name*," she repeats. I swallow. I try

Chapter 5

Every day is the same. We awake with the first glowing streaks of light, stand in the cold for roll call, rush to the main barracks for our meager portion of bread and soup, and walk the miles to the factory where we shiver in our thin blouses and skirts even in the middle of summer.

One day, I am sitting at my machine quietly working on my fifteenth uniform within the hour. To my left are the uniforms I have finished with collar and buttons, to the right another stack of perhaps twenty which await. As I set the bobbin moving with my foot on the pedal, I suddenly feel the old hunger return. This time it does not pass, but grips me like a savage claw at the heart of my diaphragm. Before I have time to lift myself from the seat, a thin stream of yellowish liquid shoots out of my mouth. Frau Helga, twitching and grinning her terrible smile, comes running toward me on her thick legs. Before she reaches me, as if from heaven, I feel a long arm grasp my shoulder from behind.

Gizella calls me a dirty cow and rushes me to one of the toilets. For a moment, I think she is going to put my head in the slimy waste,

not to look at the thick blon
shadow her eyes.

"Blima. Blima Weisstuch."

"Where are you from, Blima

"Dombrowa, Madam."

She considers this a moment.

"Dombrowa. I have not heard
town."

I sit frozen before the machine, una
take up the collar.

"Can you sew, Blima Weisstuch?" s
asks, her voice lower.

I nod, even though it is clear that I
haven't a single notion of how to proceed.
She stretches her massive hand forward as I
ready myself for the pull at the neck.
Incredibly, she begins to regulate the bobbin
and fix the collar in the proper place. The
girls' heads are all down as she straightens
herself to full height and, with not another
word, walks away.

I begin to sew.

and I feel myself gagging. Instead, she releases me and with one hand delves into her deep pocket. Again, I prepare myself for the tightening of the rope, but what emerges stuns my senses so that for the first time since my arrival at Grunberg I feel a fainting spell coming on.

A chunk of thick rye bread floats before my eyes. I have not seen such bread since the holidays when Aunt Rachel would bake them special for the family.

"Blima," she says, remembering my name, "Eat this bread now." She thrusts it into my hand, and I hurriedly gobble it up. It is hard and does not have the sweet taste of the baked goods from home, but when it reaches my stomach it is at once a soothing balm. Gizella waits until I have swallowed fully and proceeds to throw water on me as I scrub my blouse and skirt.

"Blima," she says again, "where is your mother?"

I feel the tears well up in my eyes. I had not thought of my mother in months, submerging the image of her face deep within me, along with my own fears.

Gizella bends toward me, taking my face between her long fingers, and for the first time since I am here, I see kindness in someone's eyes.

"Here, I will be your mother," she says, and kisses me on the top of my head. I cannot quite comprehend what she has told me, and I can only stare, stunned, into her blue eyes.

Gizella pushes me out, screaming again, "Dirty Jew, sick cow. Next time you will really learn your lesson!" I sit down in my place where they have added more cloth to the pile on the right, and like the machine I have become, I pick up the next item.

From that day forward, I receive a portion of bread from Gizella's deep pockets. I thrust it into the space between my breasts, beneath the cherished photos which I still carry with me, and later consume the prize in the toilet area. Once or twice, when a girl becomes particularly ill or gaunt-looking back in the barracks, I slip her the bread I had saved, telling her that I had kept my portion from the morning. Glad to satisfy her hunger, she never asks questions.

The commandant of our barracks, whose name we never knew but whom we called *Herr*, or mister, for her masculine ways, has a cruel habit. Just as the last shift of workers arrives and we are all falling into our beds, she stands at the door of the barracks, holds up a large red apple so that all can see, and bites

slowly into it. It is a difficult thing to explain
to those who sleep at night with full bellies
how this simple act can be a form of torture.
But for us girls who once knew the sweetness
of an apple, the sight is what a fantastic mountain view might be like to a man regaining his
vision after years of blindness. Some of us turn
away, but as we press our ears into the straw,
we can still hear the crunch and imagine the
taste of the juice on our tongues. Those of us
who do look see her peel the apple slowly, letting the red skin slide off the whiteness like a
party ribbon undone from a package, lazily
curling to the ground. We see the apple slowly diminish to its core, which she passes to
Otto, who attacks and finishes it in a gulp.
Then Otto approaches the skin on the floor,
sniffs once, and swiftly sucks that in, too.

One night after Herr Commandant bites
into her apple, she is abruptly called away,
leaving with Otto and the apple still in hand.
The ribbon peel lies on the floor twisted in
circles like a bright red rose. There is perhaps
a minute of silence, a tightly packed silence of
concentration such as the minute before a
child is born or a man is put into the earth.
Then perhaps a dozen girls dive upon the
floor in the same instant, pulling the apple
rose apart. There is a scratching of faces, tear-

ing of clothes, pushing and twisting as each girl tries to get her share of the peel. Who knows, perhaps I would have been among them if not for the extra bit of bread I hid away each day? The peel is devoured immediately by some, while others climb hurriedly up into their bunks to save their treasure, hiding it for now within the blades of straw. A girl named Lydia, though, remains on the floor on hands and knees, trying to insert a thin finger between the planks from which a sliver of peel peeks like a tiny worm raising its head to the sun. The rest of us are too astonished to cry out when the door silently opens and the sole of Herr Commandant's boot slams onto the girl's open hand. Just as quietly she releases the leash holding Otto. The dog goes for Lydia's arm as she tries to roll herself into a small ball. Her screams ring through the barracks while the rest of us remain fixed as stone, our mouths set in grim lines, our eyes dry as sand. When the screaming stops, the commandant says this should be a lesson to us, and pulls Otto out through the door.

After fifteen or twenty minutes, the wounded girl manages, with the help of Clara and the others, to get up off the floor. She looks down at the planks of the floor, now blotchy with patterns of dark red. I can see a long scratch stretch from the temple to her mouth. Her mangled arm hangs loosely as Clara tries to bandage the open gash with her own skirt. The girl whimpers as she climbs up to her cot, and the rest of us turn over and try to sleep. Not that night, nor for many nights after, do any of us touch, or even have a taste for, the short red peels buried within the straw.

Clara is inconsolable. It is she who marked Lydia with the scratch. It is she who is responsible for snatching the longest peel from her hand. It is she who caused Lydia to search between the planks for the tiniest scrap. It is she who allowed her friend and coworker to be caught and viciously attacked. And it is she who caused Lydia to be selected for the next transport to an even more brutal forced-labor camp. I try to tell her to be iron, that Lydia is strong still and will survive whatever is placed before her. Does she not remember the dozens of uniforms our friend completed every day? Surely, Lydia will find her way out of the darkness.

One morning, Clara does not get up for roll call. She is quiet in the straw, but I know the reason. She hopes to be punished, sent to the camp where Lydia is. But she forgets Herr

Commandant, who stands at the door with a salivating Otto at one side and the vicious whip at the other. I cannot be silent.

"Myer!"

The cry comes from my mouth the second I make up my mind to utter it, and all eyes turn toward me. Myer is Clara's five-year-old brother, confined to a wheelchair. My cry has its desired effect. At the thought of her brother, Clara resolutely steps down from the bunk and takes her place with the rest of us. Herr Commandant casts me an evil look, and Otto emits a low growl, but neither advances toward me. The only movement in the barracks is my thumb, which trembles involuntarily against my side.

I am a good worker, and the fabric flies like a hummingbird from pile to machine to floor. My small foot flies upon the pedal until I am one with the machine. Without a word, Frau Helga grasps each finished pile and carries it to a table in the center of the room. Her lack of comment is equal to praise, and I know that my value as a worker seals my security tighter each day. Sometimes, when each machine is occupied with the arrival of more workers, I am placed with the finishers. Here too my fingers learn to fly as I sew trimmings and cuffs in place. I am iron, I say to myself.

It is not my value as a worker, but Gizella's affection for me that keeps my mind alert and my heart at a steady beat. Once, I ask her why she has chosen to help me and not the others. She smiles and shrugs. It is my small stature, a will that she can see behind my eyes, she does not know. She confides that she is a Catholic and does not understand this irrational hatred of Jews. Yet, what choice does she have but to be here? I think she helps me because of her obligation to humanity.

Chapter 6

For three years I hang on, surviving. But each day I feel will be the last before the door to freedom opens, for sometimes I hear the bombings from the Russian armies drawing closer. While there is a thin sense of relief, of impending light, there is also a feeling of dread. I worry that we, too, will be blasted to oblivion along with our enemies.

There is a fire over the mountains on the day Gizella takes me aside and, along with a piece of bread, hands me the photographs I gave to her long ago for safekeeping.

"Blimala," she whispers, "Tomorrow will come a transport, and you will be on it."

"Where? Why? Where am I to go? Is my work not good enough, Gizella?" I ask, feeling each beat of my heart through my chest. She takes my arm and runs her fingers across the numbers on it.

"No, Blimala, your work is perfect, of course. But the military wants to evacuate this place. They will be sending all of us away, even me."

"But, without you, Gizella, what will become of me?" I sob into a handkerchief, ashamed to be crying tears over this woman who is not my mother.

"Do not worry, dear daughter," she says, "We will find each other after the war, for this nightmare will be at an end soon. I feel it in my bones." She embraces me as some of the girls working nearby catch sight of us, but Gizella seems not to care. The stains from my tears are still on my shirt the next day when we line up for the journey to the German concentration camp, Bergen-Belsen.

As we set out, a frosty stillness hangs in the air. I hear one of the officers give the date to another: January 21, 1945. The mountains, and with them Gizella, fade into the distance as we march into the forest. In another time, this passage would have been an adventure, and the lovely scenery would have infused us with a sense of wonder. Instead, we moved ahead without much thought or feeling, walking shadows of the persons we have once been.

Our journey is longer than the last by many days, and each day brings a new horror. Of food there is little or none, and our only nourishment comes from dry leaves or nuts left unburied by squirrels. When we are lucky, it snows, and we take piles of it in both hands, pushing the white ice into our mouths, drinking in its sweetness. By day, we walk on broken shoes, some of us on pieces of cloth that we wrap around our ankles. By night, we sleep on sheets of ice, which, warmed by the heat of our bodies, turn to pools of water before we wake. Those of us who no longer have the strength to walk, fall. Those of us whose skin trembles with the cold and whose heads are consumed by the fire of illness also fall. Others who aren't sure if they can stand or keep pace are shot. Sometimes, when the guards become bored and wish to taunt us, they make us walk a straight line, a near impossibility. They shoot bullets on either side of the line and mock the losers, the ones who collapse and are then shot to death. Other guards amuse themselves by having us run races. Then they force the losers to dig ditches for the dead. The worker who throws the last body in the ditch joins the dead with a sudden shot to the back.

For women, it is particularly difficult, as the male guards constantly remark lustfully on our breasts and thighs. We hear stories of rape, sadistic torture of girls as young as nine. But we here do not worry on that count, for starvation has robbed us of our monthly bleeding, and our skins have acquired a sickly ashen hue. My breasts too have shrunken, as I find myself tightening the bindings that hold the pictures to my chest, tighter and tighter. We were once men and women, but what we are now I cannot tell.

Sometimes, there is not the time to bury the bodies, and we march past them, trying not to look. I pass one sister coaxing another off the ground, a son urging his father to eat a piece of saved bread, a mother holding back the hair of a sick daughter as she heaves yellow water into the earth. As for me, I walk with the stars and the saplings as my only companions. Clara and the others have disappeared, and I tell myself it is good to be alone.

And I am alone, for even the fear that has been my silent friend all these years has deserted me. It walked off one day with a frightened young girl named Magda who was thrust into the position of *kapo*, group leader. Magda dared look a soldier in the eye and was seized one night in the woods as she urinated into a dirt hole right next to me. I could have been the one taken, but it was Magda who left, and in the darkness of the leafy trees, my fear slipped silently into the shadows. As I watched the ruddy-faced boy-soldier soon emerge alone from the forest, rubbing his hands and spitting hard into the ground, I knew what I had to do. What I had to do was live. Live just one more day.

Eleven days and nights we march, and we arrive in Bergen-Belsen on the twelfth day.

There is no sense of joy, no dancing except for the ones gone mad. Madness, of course, is a sensible response when the world is turned on its head. The mad ones dance as we enter the doors of another prison. No joy. But a sense of completion, yes. Perhaps now, after all, we can sleep.

I am sent to Camp C, in this place where I later learn there are a total of thirty-two blocks holding a thousand prisoners each. There is no work in this holding camp, which is just as well, for I am beyond exhaustion. Although I yearn for a change of clothes, desperately wanting to feel something clean against my skin, I find only a pair of cotton socks and slide them onto my numbed and swollen feet. I look around at the breathing skeletons surrounding me in this place where only the mad have the capacity to laugh or cry. None are young and none are old in this place called Bergen-Belsen. Few seem even alive.

No one seems to be talking much. But I notice that some of those already here have big bellies and round cheeks, so perhaps there is a meal to be had, after all. But I soon hear the woman next to me say that starvation has caused bloating in most of the inmates, and food here is scarcer than even the places from which we came. I stretch myself against my portion of floor and sleep for days.

I wake to scratching noises and turn to see a mouse sniffing at my behind. I jump up and run; I don't know where. No one seems to notice me, so I find another piece of floor and cautiously ease myself down again. But a stench so foul that it is indescribable fills my nose, making breathing difficult. Yet I do sleep for I don't know how long until, in a dream, I hear my name whispered.

"Blima . . . Blima, wake up."

Perhaps it is Clara or the Devil himself. Fighting sleep, I open my eyes wearily. I see proud dark eyes in a gaunt face. I see my sister-in-law Ruschia.

Chapter 7

I thought I had no tears to cry. But I was wrong. The water flows from my eyes in rivulets, for I had already forgotten what it was, even for a moment, to be happy. Ruschia has not the strength to embrace me, but stands at my side, smiling silently. When I can no longer bring forth tears, she sinks down next to me.

"Blima, is it really you?" she whispers. I look into the face I loved so well and see then that, yes, it is Ruschia, but not the Ruschia I had known. Not only because I can see the bones protruding from beneath her blouse, her round eyes sunken into a face covered with red blotches, but there is something gone from her essence. I know, instinctively, that she will never be the same. I do not realize it yet, but neither will I.

"What happened to you, Ruschia? Those marks on your face and arms . . ." She looks down at her arms and shrugs.

"Typhus. It comes from the lice and fleas and itches like anything."

"My poor sister-in-law! How did you ever get that?"

"Almost everyone here has it, or has

something. Let me tell you, the diarrhea is worse."

I cringe. "Why so much sickness? How does this happen, Ruschia?"

Again she shrugs her shoulders. "It is the bodies. The crematoria are full; there are hundreds, perhaps thousands here. Haven't you smelled the stench?" I remember not being able to breathe. I do not smell it as much now. Have I so soon become accustomed to the stink of death?

I tell her I have learned to be a good worker on the sewing machines, and ask if there are any in this place.

"Work?" she snorts. "We carry things from the kitchens; the men dig ditches, always too slowly, for the dead. But mostly we work to stay alive. We can do no more."

"And what of Mama and Papa, Adele, and the rest? What of Victor and the girls?" Ruschia makes a sweeping motion with one hand.

"Gone, vanished, to where—God knows. Victor, they took him from his bed. I had to bribe someone to get him to work in a warehouse. After that, I do not know."

"And your daughters, Ruschia? Where are they?" Ruschia buries her face in her blotchy hands, but does not cry.

"Off the trains they pulled us. The dogs barking, the people running, there was such shouting. I had them each by the hand, and they didn't even know anything. They were pushed along with the other children. All the children were crying. There was moaning, there was . . . Oh, God knows . . . I would have gone with them. I would have." I picture my nieces, and then I remember my pictures. I place my hand underneath my shirt, loosen the bindings, and hand Ruschia the pictures.

She spreads them out before her and looks at them as if she were seeing ghosts, and perhaps she is.

"You kept these . . . how?" I tell her of Gizella, the angel who saved me and our memories.

"If not for her, I would not be alive. So many are not . . . But, Ruschia, how do you come to be here?"

"Will, I suppose," she sighs, and proceeds to tell me of her work filling powder for guns in Auschwitz. She, too, was a good worker. She was not sent off to die with those who could not earn their keep.

"When my legs could stand no longer, I would bind them tightly to cut off the blood each night. Eventually, they had to take me to the infirmary. I think in this way, I was saved.

For what, I am not sure."

"What do you think happened to the others, Ruschia?" I ask, "Do you think—"

She cuts me off. "I do not think. And you should not think, either," she warns, then points to a woman hugging herself in a corner. "They are the ones who think. If you think, you go mad."

Ruschia is right. I can no longer think about anyone but myself. Here. Breathing and alive.

Ruschia struggles to put one arm around my shoulders.

"We are all orphans," she says.

Nibble a twelfth of a loaf of bread and take a sip of water. Slowly, slowly, until there is none left.

Ruschia is right; the business of staying alive is enough to keep us busy throughout the day. What lessons do you learn in Bergen-Belsen? You learn to stay away from the kitchens because of the sadistic Nazi officer, Herta, who beats the girls with a wooden stick as they carry their meager portions. You learn to shrivel into yourself like an old woman when the doctor comes by looking for victims for his gynecological experiments. You learn to eat your food slowly and save your water so you don't get diarrhea. You learn not to panic when an epidemic breaks out and Kramer, the head of the camp, cuts off the food supply, yelling his slogan, "If you don't eat, you don't shit!" You learn to push the hatred down into the depths of your soul when you hear that the guards have taken for themselves all but 10 of the 150 kilograms of chocolate sent by the Red Cross for the young ones. You learn how to quickly snatch the socks off a man when the breath has left him. You learn not to cry out when you take your pot of urine outside and see rats eating the faces of the dead, while some bodies are still moving within the piles. You learn not to be appalled when you hear of the cannibalism, of men eating the hearts and livers of the dead. These are the lessons of war that you learn.

April 15, 1945. Ruschia is asleep at her spot below a window. She is awakened suddenly and looks out to see fires coming from all directions, and people running about, screaming. It is the end of the world, she concludes. There has been no food now for six days, and the ground is empty of its supply of turnips. There have been rumors that this is the day the camp is to be evacuated, and since there is nowhere else to go, the talk is that they plan to line the remaining prisoners up and machine gun them at 3 p.m. But it seems too early yet. "Well," she says to me, "I can no longer walk, so if they want to shoot me, they'll have to do it here." She wakes her sister, Sophie, who comes running to my barracks.

I follow Sophie outdoors, and at first think that I have indeed gone insane. I see fire trucks and water being sprayed everywhere, but I see also something else. Potatoes on the ground. We run around grabbing as many as we can; Ruschia, who is too sick to walk, crawls on all fours. The sun comes out, bright and full, and right there in camp fires we cook the plump gifts from the earth.

A British general stands on top of a jeep and tells us we have been liberated. We sit down and eat our potatoes.

PART III

DAYLIGHT

Chapter 1

I am alive. In the midst of the chaos, confusion, the countless dead, I know just one thing. I am alive.

How do I say what I felt? It is as if I alone am standing in a hole with a bright full sun pouring into me, warm, secure. If I venture out, I will be consumed. How can I live whole with thoughts each day of my mother, my father, my sister, all my dearest friends? I have escaped the fires of the Nazi crematoriums, but do I have the will left to move into the future? For now, I stand in this hole, in this new light called freedom. And I am alive.

The guards are led away, with rifles at their backs. They are forced to carry the naked bodies, two holding each man or woman by the ankles and wrists, and swing them into ditches as big as towns. I think that the act is a double sacrilege, a murder and the killer's touch upon a holy being, but there is no other way. There are so many bodies.

Finally, the job is completed by men on trucks who scoop up the bodies like so much gravel and pour them into the ditch, arms and legs flailing, once men and women, now corpses falling upon each other. I do not want to look, but like the moth drawn to the flame, I am compelled to record the sight with my own eyes. My sister, Adele, could be in such a ditch, or my brother Kalman.

When the Red Cross comes with the food, we rush upon it. Never, we think, have our eyes seen so much food—such beauty! We push into each other, competing for a place in the front where soup is being distributed. We have forgotten politeness, for our lessons learned in the camp say you eat or you die. But Ruschia holds me back.

"Slowly, Blima," she says. "A bit of bread and water only, for we will surely get sick from stomachs filled too soon." And, as always, she is right, for those who have the huge bowls of thick vegetable soup soon become ill, and the stench and moans again fill the camp.

We are all together now, Ruschia, her sister Sophie, and I. And when we finally lift our heads, we find we are in, of all places, the military barracks, with white pillows under our heads, and soap with which to wash our hands. It is not *Judenseif*, as we fear—soap made from the bones of the dead—but American soap, packaged with a name on the top. We have kerchiefs to warm our heads against the wind, and coats with buttons for the cold. We can talk to each other and say whatever we like. Mostly, we just say thank you a hundred thousand times to the British soldiers who have young, tanned, disbelieving faces. To each other, we say nothing.

They march the guards away, rifles at their back. I see one female guard and remember how she sliced a woman's arm with the edge of a wooden stick, and how the blood erupted fast and red as if from a volcano. And I see a guard named Erich, climbing grim-faced into a truck. I remember how he stepped on a boy's hand. The boy's crime was falling asleep on a space of floor on which the guard wanted to pass. When the boy cried out, Erich kicked him in the gut. We would have killed the guards with our bare hands, sure of God's pardon, if only we had the strength. We turned away instead.

Ruschia is sicker than we know, and there

is a problem with her legs. The doctors from the Red Cross come and examine her, and they tell her there is no choice but to take her to Sweden for an operation. But she will not go.

"What if Victor comes for me?" she says. No one argues with her. She has already lost too much.

Some say it is a miracle that we survived. The British, our liberators, are kind, but they stand back a little bit, as if we are not from this world. And truly, we think the same ourselves. When we walk, it is as if we are toddlers taking our first steps. When we speak, we are silent at first, for we have yet to learn the language of free men. When we drift to sleep, it is with the anticipation of rest, not the nightmares that haunt our souls in our dreams. All of this the British soldiers, the Americans, and even the Russians now see. In Bergen-Belsen alone, they find 17,000 of us. Thousands are dying daily, liberated only for death.

How can you hate a child just because he is a Jew, the soldiers ask. How can you destroy a people for their beliefs? How can one individual hate another so that he treats him more savagely than one would treat a dog?

So, the miracle is that any survive at all, they say. But for me, the miracle is that we find each other.

Chapter 2

A woman comes to the camp looking for her husband. She has a narrow face and brownish-red hair; she wears a white button-down shift with little pink flowers on it, suitable for the summer months that have now arrived. Like many, she has already had a doctor erase the hated numbers on her arm, but by the lost expression of her eyes and the tenseness in her brow, we can tell she was a prisoner like us.

"I have word that my Moishe is staying here," she says to anyone who will listen, "Moishe Abramowitz—he was last in the Birkenau camp, maybe you know him? A small man with thinning hair who is a carpenter by trade . . . Ahh," she adds, frustrated, "he should be here. What can one do without pictures? Moishe Abramowitz, a quiet man, a carpenter. . . ." A group of Jews gathers around the woman, as they do with other searchers, almost on a daily basis now.

"*Oy!*" exclaims one man suddenly, scratching his bald head. He is a stooped man who walks with a limp. He looks to be about sixty, though he is probably no more than forty years of age.

"Moishe, maybe I know such a man. Just last week, I think—"

The woman grasps him by the collar of his shirt and pulls him to her. "Can it be you know my Moishe? Is he here, for sure? Oh, God!" The man bobs his head up and down, mutters to himself. He taps his head again.

"There is a Moishe who is, yes, a quiet man and . . . but a carpenter? I am not sure . . ." Then, releasing himself from the woman, he says, "Wait . . . wait just a small minute." He walks away as quickly as one can with a limp, as the woman pulls at her hair with anticipation. Before long, before even the man reappears, we see a short, stocky man running toward us.

"Yetta!" he screams out, and before she can embrace him, the two begin to cry.

Many such reunions have taken place in the camps, and many disappointments as well. As for us, our family has grown to include Ruschia's grown niece and nephew, as well as two of our three male cousins. They are looking for their youngest brother, for they have had word that he is alive. Everybody, it seems, is looking for someone.

Much later, as another night of wondering descends upon us, we invite Moishe and Yetta to a game of cards and begin to ask our questions. Time and curiosity have unlocked our mouths, and the words spill forth bluntly, without polite preliminaries.

"Have you seen my aunt, a big woman with short gray hair?"

"Do you know my brother, tall, blond?"

"I have a sister. She was in Auschwitz . . . maybe . . . ?"

The couple listen patiently, always touching each other, a hand on a shoulder or atop a head, watching only each other's eyes as they speak. They are reunited lovers, but also grieving parents.

"Perhaps you know my husband, Victor Weisstuch?" Ruschia asks hesitantly. The man, Moishe, straightens up, and for the first time he turns his eyes away from his wife.

"Victor? Why, he and I were in the camp together, Buchenwald . . ." The breath escapes Ruschia's lips audibly, and before she has time to ask, Moishe exclaims, "Yes, yes, my sister, the last time I saw Victor he was alive." They were together, he goes on to say, when Buchenwald was liberated, and they later stayed in the American camps. Victor had learned what had happened to Ruschia and their two little girls, and he had little hope that any of them had survived the flames of Auschwitz. His only real hope was to find his one sister, Blima, who was taken away so early. There was joy in my heart to hear that Victor was alive! But Ruschia looks down at her still legs.

"How can I go to him," she says quietly, her words more a statement than a question.

"He will come to you," I assure her.

Two days later, we receive more good news. We are looking at the new lists, just released by the Red Cross: names, age, birthplace of those found alive. We eagerly scan the names, black on white, black on white, our eyes flickering like snapping camera shutters over each one. And then our eyes set upon a bright ruby within dark clouds. "Kalman Weisstuch."

"Your brother lives!" Ruschia cries out, clasping my hand. I close my eyes, and for the first time in years I let my youngest brother's image appear before me. Kalman, with his dark curly hair and laughing dimples. Kalman, his mother's favorite. But it could not be possible. He was so young, before his bar mitzvah even. And yet, there on the paper is his name. Kalman Weisstuch. Alive.

Our second wave of good news overtakes us only weeks later as summer's heat begins to cool. Another group of survivors arrives from Warsaw. There is a man with his two young girls whom he hid in the home of a blessed Christian family for the duration of the war. He had heard that his wife, a woman named Ruthie, was staying here with us. No one knows her. Perhaps she is one who had been taken to the hospital in Sweden, someone said. We have a hope for this, anyway. The man heaves a huge sigh, as if he has done this many times before, then, looking at the two tired girls by his side, asks if we do not mind if they rest here. Of course not, we answer, who could object, God forbid! That night, we sit again outdoors drinking glasses of tea with apples, watching a half moon sail forward in the gray darkness. The man tells us that he too knew Victor and that, in fact, my brother and a cousin are already on their way to this very place. Ruschia and I look at each other through lowered lids, not wishing to show our joy in the face of the man's personal misery. But our eyes, though shielded, are smiling.

Chapter 3

Victor arrives a day before Rosh Hashanah, the Jewish New Year, his cousin with him. How do I have words to express such a joy? Ruschia's and my happiness is matched only by that of Victor himself who, having lost half his stomach and gained two dark circles under his eyes, beams nonetheless. When he embraces me and stares into my face, it is good to see again eyes that match my own. After a silence that is richer than words, he describes how he worked from the first light until the shroud of night, bolting Nazi rifles together or carrying boxes beyond one hill to the next. He tells us too how he would stand tall and puff out his chest each time there was a selection of those who remained healthy enough to work. He asks how it is possible that we are here, so Ruschia tells of the trick she conceived in binding her legs, and I tell him of my angel, Gizella.

"When we are all together, I will find her and thank her," I say.

"Oh, sister, I fear we *are* all together, Mama, Tata, all of them in the house were taken at the same time. And, *oy*, you know the story. ... Our parents, my God, I am sure went to the fires, and the swine had no use for children. Our sister Miriam no doubt went with her children, in her foolish stubbornness."

He turns as he hears Ruschia murmuring under her breath, "Maybe it was not stubbornness, but because she is a mother, as I once was . . ."

Victor kisses Ruschia's forehead and cheeks.

"No, it was for you to live," he says, adding, "but my brothers and sisters, they had no luck . . ." I open my mouth to speak when the image of our family sitting in the parlor, Tata with his newspaper, Mama sewing, and the rest talking, playing games, at once normal and precious, flashes like a camera shot before my eyes.

Victor leans over and gives my arm a tight squeeze.

"I am sorry for you, Blimala. Adele, who was your constant companion, and your own twin, Froyim . . . do you remember how he protected you? . . . Ah, even your Smulke, always so headstrong—I hear he was shot trying to escape on a death march in the forest . . ." He lowers his voice. "All, wiped away with one hand."

I can do nothing but look down at my feet, warmed now by white anklets and simple loafers. If I gaze backward, I tell myself, I will surely be consumed by the fires of the past, so I must stand here beneath the sun. Stand here with the remnants of my family, my one beloved brother. . . . Oh, what was I thinking just a moment ago? What was I about to say when . . . and then it comes to me, tumbles out of my mouth in a rush.

"Victor, our brother, Kalman, is alive!"

Victor's eyes open incredulously. He breathes out the words, "Blima, it cannot be . . . he was too young." But Ruschia confirms my words, telling Victor about the list and that she saw only a few days ago that Kalman Weisstuch from Dombrowa was on it. Victor shakes his head, disbelieving, and then, strangely, he begins to sob like a small child. Ruschia, Sophie, and I cannot bear the sight of a man crying, especially a man such as Victor, and soon we are all weeping. I am not sure if we are crying in our joy about Kalman or in sorrow for the ones we have lost, but the release of tears, so long forbidden, revives us like a sudden spring rain. We cry for a very, very long time, and when we are done, Victor pledges to look for our brother as soon as the holiday is over.

And such a holiday it is! Never has there been a New Year such as this, nor I suspect will there ever be another. We put on the best of our charity clothes, and the men gather together in a tent that we use for a synagogue. By a miracle, one of many, someone is able to secure a Torah, and as it is carried outdoors, we tap our prayer books against the Holy Scrolls as tears fill our eyes. From afar, we women prepare fish and set tables with braided *challah* bread and even some wine as we watch the men, each bent and swaying, head covered by a prayer shawl. They are not the prayer shawls received at bar mitzvahs, but new ones signifying a new chance, a renewal of life. The prayers go up to God in a series of moans and tears, enough to pierce heaven itself. Some of the older men and women collapse, struck by the raw emotion of the day. But not I, for since the day I left my home, I have had not one fainting spell. God has blessed me with a new-found strength, and this is just one of the things which I thank Him for on this day. I tend to the weak with soft words and a steady hand, and dole out pieces of apples and honey to the few young ones who wait for the treats, shuffling their feet impatiently.

At Kol Nidre, that most beautiful service on the night before Yom Kippur, we sing with a passion that would rival the voices of angels.

Oh, and when I look up, I can see the clouds parting slowly in the purple sky, and as surely as I know there is a God, I can hear Him listening with each murmur of the wind. The next day, our leather shoes and belts removed as required by Law and prayer books in hand, we stand once more before God. And although one day is not enough for our multitude of prayers, we stand close, women on one side, men on the other, and, with our fists pounding our chests, say aloud our public, our most private yearnings. *Forgive us, Oh Lord, for eating the unkosher, for our blasphemy, for our traitorous ways against our brethren and our enemies, for the foulness of mouth, our stiff-neckedness, our pride...Oh, Lord, forgive, forgive...* And, for the first time in my life, I say the prayer for the dead of blessed memory: *God, remember the souls of my beloved, and bind them with the blessed souls of Abraham, Jacob, Isaac, Sarah, Rachel, Rebecca, Leah. . . .* We thank Him too for the multitude of blessings bestowed upon us, and the possibility of the extra years that surely will flow from life. As the darkness paints its first stars against the sky, we leave our tent with voices hoarse and spirits filled with conviction.

Outside, Victor, Ruschia, Sophie, the

cousins, and I kiss each other, but none of us makes a move back to quarters, for our stomachs do not call to us in hunger. Instead, we are content to stand and watch the Jews all around us, walking home as free men who have just completed a Yom Kippur fast on the soil of their enemies.

Chapter 4

Victor leaves to find Kalman, but returns alone after only a few days. He is distraught, and believes now he has lost his youngest brother a second time. He tells how he met a man on the train to Munich. The man's words, he tells us, were as sour as his face.

"He knew Kalman from a work camp when they were together in the salt mines," Victor says. "There was a selection, and Kalman, along with his own brother, was taken to Dachau. And there, the brother tells him, he witnessed Kalman selected to die."

"But the list!" I scream. "The list tells us that Kalman lives!"

"Oh, sister," answers my brother, exhausted, "the one thing worse than despair is hope followed by disappointment. We must find our happiness in each other."

But it is Ruschia who will not let the matter rest.

"No, Victor, you must continue to look. You know how quick young Kalman always was. Perhaps . . . perhaps . . ."—she looks for the words in the air—"he jumped from one line to the other, or ran down a road unobserved. You must go back. But this time, I will go with you, if you can wait just a few days."

Ruschia is sufficiently recovered to walk, although the doctors caution that an operation will still be necessary. She sets out with Victor, who admits that if it weren't for her, he would not have the strength for the trip. I remain behind to cook and care for the others, but already I am planning my mission to find Gizella, my savior.

And five days later, when they return, Victor tells it to me this way:

"We were just off the train, walking into the city of Munich. Everyone seemed to be running here and there, like ourselves, looking for family. People, some dressed in the finest garb as if there had never been a war, others in flimsy jackets, confused, and it is these whom I approached. I repeated the name of my brother until it came from my mouth without thinking. I must have looked frantic, like a madman, I don't know.

"Finally, a tall man with graying hair came up to me and placed his hand on my shoulder. 'Don't look so disturbed, my friend,' this kind man said. 'We all have our sorrows, but you must remain strong and not get your expectations too high.' Then, looking into my face, he thought he recognized me, but after we talked awhile, we realized that we had been in different camps, and this was not possible. I told him my name. He said it sounded somewhat familiar, but how? Then, suddenly, as if a bell had rung, the man stood erect and said he had just met a boy of the same name. He had been talking to him as they came out of the station not five minutes ago. 'Why,' I exclaimed, 'that is my brother!' Without replying, the man pointed to the crowd of people a few feet ahead. Already I was running, screaming his name, and then I saw the curly dark hair turning around, and the dimpled face of a boy much taller but skinnier. Oh my sister, it *was* a miracle!"

Not only was our Kalman alive, but he was well, too, and had been staying in a displaced persons camp outside of Munich. He would be on his way in less than one week when, finally, two brothers and their sister would be reunited.

I cannot recall having been happier, and I now understand what I never did before. Before the war, with my family of seven siblings, I was content, and I could have been so for the rest of my life. But when the fabric of contentment has been ripped apart in such a way, and when one experiences the gaping hole that is loss, only to find again something of what you had before, that is true happiness.

When Kalman finally appears, he and

Victor and I fall upon each other, locking together in a steel embrace, links in a chain of family. As I look at Kalman, his face so serious, with a maturity come too early, I know there is a purpose to my having been saved. And now, more than ever, I am glad that I was.

We continue our lives at the camp, for many are still ill, and others, like ourselves, do not yet have the strength or desire to venture forth. Kalman returns to his home outside Munich, but visits often, returning with copies of *Our Way*, an official newspaper produced by the Central Committee of the Liberated Jews in Bavaria. We spend our days looking through the lists of survivors and reading the testimonies of other Jews from the camps and the ghettos who had undergone atrocities even we could not imagine. Kalman also often ventures into the center of the camp to listen to the political leaders who lecture there. What he likes best are the Zionists who criticize the Brits for limiting the number of Jews who move to Palestine. He tells us that in July he even marched with other displaced persons to the site in Munich where Hitler rose to power, to sing the Palestinian anthem and say the prayer for the dead. But not all of us are swept along by this political fever to establish a Jewish state. When we beg our teenaged brother to join one of the camp's soccer teams or continue his studies in one of the many small schools sprouting everywhere like flowers, he points to the barbed wire which still surrounds the camp and asks us if we feel free.

"It is no different," he says, "throughout the cities in Germany where the citizens, without guns or dogs, still curse and spit on us as we walk the streets!"

I have but one thought, and that is to find my Gizella. Finally, my patient search is rewarded. I receive a note from someone who knows a woman in Munchberg, a woman who lived with Gizella before the war. Victor accompanies me on the train. As I watch the countryside fly past me like a foggy dream, I recall the last time I boarded a train and the icy fear which gripped my heart. I am confused and do not know what I will say to Gizella once I set my eyes upon her, but I know that I will never leave her again. Of that, I am quite sure.

Chapter 5

Etta Danhaus's apartment reflects the neatness and order of one who is accustomed to doing things her own way. Shades resembling white doilies are hung primly over sparkling windows. Hot tea is served from a polished silver tea set placed on a round table covered by a white cotton tablecloth trimmed with purple fringe. On the wall over the table hangs a large simple wooden cross, flanked by pictures of the German countryside. I can see how Gizclla would have fit well into this place, so ordered, so neat, so far removed from the insane chaos of Grunberg.

"I trust you have not had an unpleasant journey here," says Frau Danhaus, bending slowly to pour the tea into little cups of china. The appearance of this frail woman matches that of her home. She appears to be in her eighties. Her hair, a pure white, is loosely piled on the back of her head and fastened with an onyx comb. She wears no makeup except for two lines of pink rouge painted on her cheekbones. She is attired in a tangerine-colored suit with huge round buttons, and as she pours, I can smell cheap German cologne. I am humbled that she considers my visit an occasion for formality. Overall, Frau Danhaus reminds me of a small sparrow, so quick are her movements. Even her voice has a chirping quality.

I assure her that my journey was most pleasant. I tell her that for many months since the war has ended, I have been driven by the desire to see my old friend. Etta eases herself into the chair opposite me.

"Ah, such tragedy. And, for what, my child, for what?" She takes a slow sip of her tea before adding a cube of sugar.

"You say you know Gizella from the factory, yes?" she inquires.

I nod, leaving my tea to cool before tasting it.

"Well, then, you know Gizella was a remarkable person from a remarkable family. Such a tragedy, yes . . ."

I strain to understand the heavy German accent. Generally my home-spoken Yiddish allows me to understand German, but not always. "I really know nothing of her family," I reply.

"Ah, so sad," she says, stirring her tea slowly. With each clink of the spoon against the cup, I feel my nerves rising with impatience.

"Please, madam . . ." I try, "I just came to

find out where she is. Perhaps you can help me?"

Frau Danhaus shakes her head briskly from side to side and bites her lip. "Of course, well, our poor Gizella was all alone in this world. She was a boarder here, in this very apartment. Small, but it suited her needs. You see, I was more than her landlady, really. And she paid me what she could for, as you know, she was a brilliant finisher, and when she worked in a factory for ladies' dresses, she actually was paid quite a handsome sum. Even before that, I knew her parents. God bless their souls, I knew them well. Her father and I grew up on this very street, only four houses apart. And her mother, so tiny, little mouth, little feet, as tiny as her husband was tall, as Gizella herself would become." The old woman begins to lose herself in her memories. "Almost comical it looked when the parents walked down the street together. Ah, but her mother, Marta, was the very breath of kindness who did not know even one bad word. Did you know Gizella's mother's father was a Jew?"

She continues, not stopping to look at my face, which turns white.

"I think that is why Gizella had such a feeling for the Jewish people, you see, knowing that she had Jewish blood as well. Of her husband, Klaus, I do not know, but certainly he was a tolerant man, not like some of the other Germans."

"What? Do you mean to say that Gizella was married?"

Frau Danhaus nods. "Surely, if only for a short time. And then, of course, the tragedy . . . "

"The war, yes, so tragic," I interrupt.

She dismisses my words with a wave, puts down her cup, and looks directly at me.

"But . . . did you not know?" she continues. "I was home right here, and I could hear the screams even from down the street. I could not even move, for I had broken my ankle only a week earlier, and I could only sit home holding my head and worrying as the sirens came closer. This was in 1933, before the problems of the Jews, and sirens were not heard every day. So you see, it was unusual. Only many hours later, when Gizella came running to my house like a wild woman, did I realize that the foul odor coming through my window contained the ashes of my friends, her parents, and her husband. They say it was probably her father smoking in the bed that caused the fire . . . ah, but what does it matter now?" The old woman rubs her eyebrows as if to wipe the picture from her memory. She takes a deep breath before resuming. "Klaus and her father worked nights in a bakery. If Gizella had not already left for her day's work, then she too would have been gone."

"And I as well," I murmur to myself, but I don't think Frau Danhaus hears.

"Poor Gizella, poor orphan," she sighs. "I had no choice but to take her in. I would have done it even without her giving me money. I would have done it for her dear parents. . . . So here we were, the two of us, and she so depressed over her losses that she miscarried the baby inside of her. She was not the person she once was, and when the war came, she left without a word. But in a way, I thought it would do her good, you know, to busy her hands, even if it was for those godless swine."

"But, excuse me, Frau Danhaus, have you seen her since the war? Has she returned, or have you had any word?" I press.

"Ah, no, my dear. Her friend—the one that had known her in the work camp—said she left one day toward the end of the war, you know, she left with the Nazi guards, but never returned. There were rumors, oh, Jesus forgive me for repeating them, that she was helping a Jewess, and was found out and shot for the deed. But, please, these are only rumors, and it is just as likely that she has left

Germany for good. I tell you, I wouldn't be at all surprised. . . . But, my dear, are you upset? I really did not mean to upset you with this gossip. My dear?" Frau Danhaus, seeing me cover my eyes with my hands, lowers her cup and bends toward me.

Glancing at my watch, I quickly jump up from the chair.

"Thank you so much for the tea, but I am sure my brother is already downstairs pacing the street with worry," I say, removing a piece of paper from my purse and handing it to her. "I ask only one more favor. Here is my name and where you may contact me should Gizella reappear. Tell her Blima is looking for her . . . her daughter, Blima."

Frau Danhaus stands, gazing at me quizzically, as I rush out the door and down the stairs. The lobby door slams behind me, and I hear a tinkling of bells as they signal the end of yet another chapter in my life.

Chapter 6

We are like Gypsies now, moving from one town to the next. We establish roots nowhere, knowing that we can never feel safe living among the Germans. Besides, we are yet fearful to separate, and find a certain peace of mind in the security of each other.

Ruschia, Victor, and I are together now wherever we go. Victor has found a little business for himself, selling silverware and such, and Ruschia has had the surgery on her legs. I keep up our living quarters as best I can, and try not to think too much about the fact that of the 58,000 people liberated from Bergen-Belsen, 30,000 have since died. If I think too much about it, the war will never end for me, and I want it to end now. So if I am not yet happy, I would say that I am content.

My brother and sister-in-law want me to marry. I am not so sure. It is not that I miss Smulke so much, and going back is impossible, anyway. But I am not sure if I can make small talk and play the role of someone's sweetheart. But they assure me that this will not be necessary as, of course, any Jewish boy will also have his difficulties. I agree, finally, because I know that I have been burden enough to my dear brother and sister-in-law. After all, I can't stay with them forever.

Our cousin is staying in Munich now, and has met somebody suitable for me. His name is Chiel, and he is from the Lodz ghetto. I do not know much about him, except that he is all alone, as are many of us now, and I learn he was something of a hero during the war. He is to arrive for the weekend, with cousins as chaperones.

Ruschia is well enough now to help me get ready. She teaches me how to make her tasty chicken soup, with the trick of putting in a spoonful of sugar for extra taste. We travel the few miles to the kosher butcher for his finest cut of brisket, and cook it in a brown gravy with many onions, lastly adding thick slices of carrots and potatoes. I am even able to find a bakery that is not quite as good as Aunt Rachel's, but has the black bread that I so love. Ruschia has also gone to the trouble of making a honey cake, and it is not even the New Year! Hours before the arrival, she trims my hair in the front and curls it just so it covers my eyebrow; then she makes me wear her coral lipstick and a touch of rouge on my cheeks. Finally, she gives me my belted blue dress on which she has sewn a big letter "B" for Blima. I am a little worried. I hope she does not want to get rid of me too fast.

They arrive at 4 p.m. on Friday, just before the beginning of Sabbath. When Chiel comes in, I notice two things about him immediately. First, he is short. Of course, he is a few inches taller than I; almost everyone is. But he does not have the commanding stature of Smulke, who would pick me up by my elbows to give me a kiss. The second thing I notice about him is his hair, which is thick, soft, and very dark. This is unusual, especially for a man of 37; many men I know have but a few strings of hair, if any, to cover their balding heads. I wonder what it would be like to put my fingers in such hair.

Everyone is appropriately silent during our meal, their eyes glancing from Chiel to me as we try to manage conversation. Chiel overly praises the meal, as I avert my eyes.

"Such a sweet soup!" "The brisket, so tasty!" "May I have another piece of that wonderful bread?" "I am so stuffed . . . maybe just another glass of tea?"

Finally, we push back our chairs, and Chiel asks if I would like to take a walk in the yard. I agree, and he holds the back screen door open for me as we go outside. The May air is brisk, and I wrap my cardigan sweater around my shoulders. He helps adjust the collar, then quickly returns his hands to his pockets.

"Look at that moon," he says, pointing beyond the branches of an oak tree. The moon is unusually round and luminous as puffs of clouds sail slowly past its face.

"Mmm . . . quite lovely," I answer. I can feel the blush rising up my face as I look back and see Ruschia, Victor, and the cousins sitting outside, cutting pieces of apple into their tea. They seem involved in conversation, but when I turn, I feel their smirks at my back.

"I am by nature not a talker," Chiel blurts out.

I come back to the moment. "Oh, well, how much can one talk anyway?" I say, looking down at my fingernails as Chiel rests against the oak tree.

"May I ask your story?" he says. I know exactly what he means. Every survivor has a story to tell, and some release it more willingly than others.

"Well, of course, as you know, it is not so easy," I answer, still looking at my fingernails. I realize that I have never told the entire story to anyone other than family; I never really had to. I begin slowly, but once I hear the sound of my own voice, I am surprised at how fast the words come. I tell him of my life working in the bakery, of my sisters and how one had

won a beauty contest, of my twin brother, my
Tata and of Mama, whom I never saw again
after the Nazis took me from the street as she
screamed and screamed my name. I tell him
about how I learned to sew and how quick my
hands became with the needle. I tell him
about my angel, Gizella, who saved me from
starvation. I tell him about being sent to
Bergen-Belsen, and meeting Ruschia who was
sick with typhus, and the tears when we
remembered her two little girls. I tell him
everything.

I feel his eyes, large and hazel, resting
upon me the whole time I speak. But when I
ask to hear of his story, he looks down on the
ground and unclasps his hands. His white
pants and shirt float momentarily in the
breeze and shimmer in the moonlight.

"My parents owned a fruit store, and my
brother Aron and I worked there with them,"
he says, his eyes never leaving the ground.
"There were also three sisters, one with two
young children, one just married, and the
youngest just a girl, sweet and quiet, with a
long sad face. My Tata, may he rest in peace,
died before the war. He went to bed one
night and simply left the world. Like a king he
died in his own bed. He was fortunate. . . ."
At this point, Chiel exhales and places his

hands on his head as if to coax the memories.

"So in the ghetto, you know, it was not so good. They closed us down almost immediately and made us work in the factories—they called them factories, but you knew they were really labor camps. I too learned the machines, but I also learned to be a smuggler of sorts, helping people find hiding places during the exportations, getting them necessities, like lamps and radios. Ah, they were all afraid of the guards patrolling the fence, but I managed. There is a good thing about being small and quick."

He flashes me a smile then, a warm smile. As I again survey his short wiry frame, I can understand why he was considered a hero.

"As I say, then, I managed. For me, the watery soup with the sausage made of horse-meat was enough. . . ." Then, dropping his composure, he lifts his arms to the sky, exclaiming, "God, only you, dear God, know our sufferings!" We are quiet then, both of us, before he resumes.

"So this is how it went. And in the end, they came for everybody, to choose victims for Auschwitz, you know. Well, the soldiers took one look at me—I was much thinner than I am now—and they pointed to the left. And just like that, they shoved me into the line for death. When I saw all the sick ones, some of the older ones too, I knew what we were there for. But the guards did not know Chiel Russak so well, and so while they were busy barking orders, I ran for the right side. No one saw, and I guess I was a little bit lucky. They tell me all together that 74,000 left for Auschwitz, and not many returned." Here, he pauses, looks over to the back porch, then takes my hand and motions for me to sit, right there on the grass by the tree.

"After the liberation, I found out they had all been gassed. My Mama, my brother and best friend, my sisters, my nieces and nephews. Only Shani, the youngest, survived. I heard she was sent to a hospital in Paris, but when I got there she had already died of food poisoning. . . . Ah, that's how life goes, I suppose."

I notice then how calmly and evenly he relates the story, but I guess it is the same for most of us. We learn to disengage ourselves. It is another story in another life.

Chiel goes on, "It was then that I realized that I was all alone, except for a few cousins." He gives me a half smile.

"When I returned from Paris, I was sick myself, quite swollen in the face. You wouldn't recognize me." He chuckles, then turns serious. "I found our old apartment, would you believe. Things all over the place, old toasters and blankets, most of it ransacked. I was looking for some pictures of the family. I had none, not one—"

I interrupt, "I have pictures. I will show you later. . . . But, oh, I am sorry, please continue."

He went on. "I searched for hours and found but one picture. Would you like to see it?"

I nod, and Chiel reaches into his pocket and removes a wallet, showing me a photograph. It is a studio picture of a handsome young boy, about twenty, with intense eyes that stare straight into the camera. He has a neatly combed head of thick black hair. It is a photograph of Chiel.

"Isn't that something?" he smiles, poking the photo as if to make it jump. "The only photograph I could find was one of myself."

We stare at the picture for many minutes before he puts it away, and we walk back toward the house, hand in hand.

Many hours later when the Sabbath candles have already gone out, Ruschia, in her nightgown, comes into the parlor where I am sitting in an armchair alone.

"So . . .?" she says, raising an eyebrow.

"I think he will do," I say.

Chapter 7

We are married on April 25, 1947. It is the same month I first was taken from Mama's home, and the same month in which I regained my freedom into a world I no longer recognized. But it is the first time in many Aprils when I can freely say that, like the grass, I too am reborn.

As I walk toward the *chupa*, the Jewish canopy, with my brother Victor supporting me on one side, and Ruschia on the other, I feel a happiness settle into my heart like nothing I have known before. It is like a piece of warm sun, soft like pudding, and glowing like a mother's touch. It is a survivor's kind of happiness, the sort one never experiences unless the worst has been felt. It feels wonderful, and I want to remain in the moment, hold still the hands of the clock, forever.

Chiel steps down hard and breaks the glass as all the people cheer, *"Mazel Tov!—good luck!"* As he lifts the veil to kiss me before God and our well-wishers, I feel myself blush. I am Chiel's wife, I am a part of someone, and I have a future. I look at my new husband and smile.

Never before do I remember being so

doted upon. All eyes are on me as the photographer snaps pictures of Chiel and me under the *chupa*, clapping hands as we dance, me sitting on a throne with my white bridal gown floating beneath me. If only Adele could see me now! Ruschia fixes my veil; it is long, multi-layered, and made of very white lace. Even Chiel's fat cousin sprays me with perfume when I walk by. As for the dress itself, it seems to belong to another, not made for one such as I. Surely it is the most stunning outfit I have ever found myself in. It has a wide petticoat and a scoop neck with puffy sleeves. I am swallowed up in its layers, and am only lacking the magic wand for the role of fairy princess. It is the first time that I, Blima, am the center of attention, adored by all. I didn't even have my mother's womb to myself. I am uncomfortable, but I like it. And yet, in the midst of my greatest happiness, there is a solemn voice reminding me: It is only for the moment, Blima. Only for the moment.

Chiel and I set up a home close to the few cousins he has. Even though we have known each other for only a few months, I learn that my intuition was right. He is a good man and a good husband. Every day he is busy at one business or another. One day he is working with deliveries at a fruit merchant's; the next he is sewing coats at a friend's textile plant. Many times, I offer to work, but he prefers that I busy myself with the cooking or planting the tomatoes and peppers on the small terrace outside our apartment. My hands, knowing only the labor of twisting fabric and pushing in the needle, feel useless, but I do not argue. I understand him. He wants to be the man, the provider, and to build our future.

While the sun shines, Chiel is quiet, letting his hands and legs do the work to carry him into his future. But at night, when the darkness seeps through the windows like a cat, his mouth pries itself open. He talks a great deal about the war and his family. This he does in the same detached way he spoke on the day we met. At other times, he is sullen, and I see the tinge of uncertainty in his hazel eyes. At these times, he holds me close to him as I feel the strength slowly seeping from my body to his.

Despite his small stature, or perhaps because of it, Chiel's virility knows no bounds. He delights openly in my breasts, my narrow waist, and slowly I feel my shyness melt away before him. He is forever my guard, scowling at men who look in my direction a little longer than they should. At least ten times each day, he asks if I love him. At these times, I take his hands and slip my fingers through his. His leg, like the trunk of a tree, feels cool and familiar next to my thigh. To be wife, sister, mother to a man still so young, yet so chastened by life, is the awesome burden to which I must yield. "Yes, my dear, I do love you," I say. And looking at that shy half smile of his, I am sure of it. That's when he promises me again that he will make our future, and it will come soon.

It comes sooner than I anticipate. One evening, Chiel comes home late from the textile plant. He is waving a telegram in his hand, and rushes to embrace me.

"Do you remember my Aunt Sifra and her husband whom I told you about? Well, finally, they have written and will sponsor us. Blimala, we are going to America!"

My heart jumps, but there is worry between my smiles. America is so far away, after all, a whole ocean to cross! A culture, a language that are a world apart, an ocean apart! And I am just learning to make my way here, in a world that I have known all my life. And, while I have hardly any family left here, I have none there at all.

But Chiel and I spend a whole evening talking, and gradually each little fear subsides. He will find a job and go to school to learn English. I will make new friends, American friends who will not hate me because I am a Jew. And how many people we will meet there, Jews and even Christians, *good* Christians, Negroes, Spanish. People from all walks of life will be in this land where the streets are paved with gold!

Victor and Ruschia come to our home. It is only a few months since we have received permission to emigrate to America, with Chiel's aunt and uncle as our sponsors. Ruschia is folding woolen blankets and handing them to me so that I can stack them neatly in the suitcase.

"To think," she says, fixing a corner of the blanket, "that by next month you will be living in your new home in America!"

"Oh, Ruschia, I am not so sure about this. After all, you and Victor and Kalman will be so far away. Who knows when we will see each other again?"

"Nonsense! Sometimes, Blima, you speak like a child," she replies, brusquely grabbing another blanket. "We will all be together quicker than you think, as soon as you make the arrangements for us. Why, even Kalman is convinced that maybe America is not so bad. Who knows, maybe he will even find an American bride!"

"Oh, I don't know . . . a whole ocean to separate us." I sit down on the bed as I feel the burning of tears in my eyes. "I know this is silly, but I feel like I am leaving Mama and Tata here, everything I have loved and known . . . "

Ruschia puts down the blanket and, taking my hand, sits down next to me. "Believe me, Blima, you are leaving ashes only behind. Their spirit," she adds, tapping my chest gently, "is here, and you can never leave that."

I gulp down my sadness, recalling the day Mama and I sat in her bedroom and how she placed her hand on my chest and said how alike we were. Ruschia continues, "As for me, I will be glad to leave any soil that still holds the Nazi footprint." She lowers her voice and squeezes my hands between her own. "Here there is no more happiness. We must build our happiness in the future."

But then she closes her eyes momentarily and pauses. "Blima, may I ask you one favor only?"

I nod, but already I am moving toward my black purse on the dresser. I remove three of the photographs and hand them to her

Ruschia runs her fingers across each picture as if she is again stroking the faces of her children. Then she quickly places them in the pocket of her skirt.

"Ruschia," I say, still sitting down, looking into the eyes of my sister-in-law and friend, "that day in Bergen-Belsen when I awoke not knowing if I would see the Devil himself, and then when I saw you—"

"I know," she answers quietly, rising as she kisses my forehead, "Let's finish packing."

The next day, as the dawn rises between the clouds, I stand shivering on the deck. Already there are lines of shadow crossing the faces of my loved ones left behind. And, still waving, I stand on tiptoes to see them. Suddenly, I feel a momentous force scooping me up and lifting me away as the water's spray beckons at my back. I look up. The day is gray, but there are glints of radiant sun as Chiel takes my hand. I turn to face the ocean and my future.

AFTERWORD

After Blima and Chiel arrived in the United States, they set up housekeeping in Brooklyn, New York. They adopted the American names of Betty and Charlie and soon had a daughter and a son. They named the children Sheindel and Yankel, after Blima's mother and Chiel's father, but called them Shirley and Jack.

The family did well in America, with Shirley becoming a writer and teacher, and Jack a lawyer. In their later years, Blima and Chiel enjoyed their grandchildren and were able to visit Israel, Italy, and Switzerland. But they never returned to Germany, a place that held so many nightmares for them.

Chiel suffered a stroke and died in 1983. Blima developed Alzheimer's disease in the mid-1990s and died in 1999. The author of this book, Shirley Russak Wachtel, is Chiel and Betty's daughter. She is a professor of English at Middlesex County College in Edison, New Jersey.